Out of the Wilderness

The Spiritual Path Hidden in Genesis

Ron Grimes

Copyright Page

Cover design by nskvsky

ISBN: 979-8-9922823-8-2 (Paperback)

First Edition under this title. This work was previously published as *Creation's Silent Path: Discovering Hesychastic Truths in Genesis* (Second Edition, September 2025).

Published by Grafted In Publishing

Printed in the United States of America

About the Cover

The cover depicts a solitary pilgrim walking a winding path into the light.

In the pages of this book, Adam's story unfolds as the journey of every soul—called out of the formless darkness and drawn toward the quiet radiance of God. The path that winds through the mountains symbolizes the hesychastic way: a gradual ascent from chaos into stillness, from fragmentation into communion, from night into the first light of dawn.

The scattered points of light surrounding the pilgrim evoke the countless thoughts that rise and fall within the heart each day, hinting at the inner work explored throughout these chapters—learning how to notice, name, and pass through one's thoughts without being carried away by them.

Thus, the image mirrors the movement traced in Genesis and developed in this book, culminating in the inner "dawn" described in Chapter Six, *"Before the Light."*

Cover image: *stylized illustration of a solitary pilgrim walking a luminous mountain path at dawn. Cover art by nskvsky.*

Dedication

To St. Jerome, whose profound respect for the Hebrew language and the Jewish context of Scripture has inspired generations to seek the truth in its original form.

CONTENTS

Preface

This book is the result of the *incubation effect*—a phenomenon we've all experienced at various points in our lives. It's that moment when several threads of study and experience, long buried in the subconscious, suddenly emerge as a beautifully complex tapestry that makes perfect sense. Years of effort and reflection coalesce, and we understand why we felt driven to undertake it all. The self-questioning—"Why am I even studying or doing this?"—finally gains meaning.

The Tapestry's Threads

Biblical Languages and Jewish Context

For me, one crucial thread began with years of studying biblical languages—Hebrew, Aramaic, and Greek—alongside the Jewish context of biblical times. Through the Israel Institute of Biblical Studies, in association with the Hebrew University of Jerusalem, I gained a deeper appreciation for the Torah, particularly the creation and Fall narratives in Genesis. I repeatedly returned to these foundational stories, sensing—though unable to fully articulate why—that they held the key to understanding the entire Bible.

Stillness and Transformation

After my conversion to the ancient Eastern Orthodox Christian faith, another vital thread emerged as I encountered *hesychasm*, a spiritual discipline of stillness and inner quiet. This practice illuminated the spiritual depth of Genesis, showing how God's light brings order to chaos—a theme reflected in the creation stories. After years of contemplation, a sudden moment of clarity—a genuine "aha" moment—revealed the deeper essence of the creation and Fall stories, becoming essential to understanding their meaning and the purpose of the Law.

Weaving the Threads Together

These threads converged to reveal the Bible's overarching message—a unified spiritual narrative. For most of my life, these truths had eluded me, but suddenly, I could see the Bible as a masterfully crafted work, with a theme introduced in Genesis and carried forward through Revelation. To fully appreciate this, I needed a new model of interpretation—one that embraced the spiritual depth hidden in the allegories.

This Book's Approach

Perspective: While accessible to all Christian traditions, many insights reflect Eastern Orthodox practices and perspectives, which will be specified when relevant.

References: Book references appear inline, eliminating the need for a separate bibliography.

Terminology: Unfamiliar terms are explained within the text, with frequently used foreign terms included in a glossary.

Style: A "casual scholarly" approach balances depth with accessibility.

Repetition as a Teaching Tool

Repetition is used deliberately throughout the book to help readers absorb complex ideas, dismantle preconceptions about the Genesis stories, and build a clearer framework for understanding. This approach is inspired by the Hebrew Bible's use of synonymous parallelism, where ideas are expressed twice for emphasis and deeper resonance.

For example, in Psalm 19:1, "The heavens declare the glory of God, and the firmament showeth His handiwork," repetition enriches meaning and creates a rhythm that draws the reader deeper into its message. Similarly, this book uses repetition not as mere restatement but as a method to guide readers toward fuller understanding, allowing key ideas to unfold gradually.

Invitation to the Reader

As you embark on this journey, I invite you to approach the Genesis narratives with fresh eyes so as to discover their rich layers of meaning that transcend time and illuminate the unified spiritual narrative of the Bible.

Introduction

The psalmist invites us to "Be still and know that I am God," but in a chaotic world, how do we find the stillness necessary to truly know Him? For centuries, people of faith have turned to the Scriptures in search of answers. As I read the Torah—the foundation of the Bible—I began to ask, "If stillness is essential for knowing God, where are its teachings woven into these ancient texts? How do they guide us toward achieving such a state?"

At first, the answers weren't obvious. The creation and Fall narratives in Genesis felt distant, cloaked in metaphor, and seemingly disconnected from the stories that followed. They appeared to function as loosely constructed preludes, condensing thousands of years into just a few chapters before shifting to the history of Abraham and his descendants.

These narratives seemed like allegorical tales presented as fictionalized history, setting the stage for Israel's actual story. At times, they even resembled poetic but overly simplistic attempts to engage with natural sciences rather than profound spiritual truths. Yet, I began to wonder if the issue was not with the text itself but with me—removed by centuries from its language and context, perhaps I was missing its deeper meaning.

Linguistic Forensics: The Role of Language

To uncover their deeper meanings, I realized I needed a different approach—one that examined the text's language, historical context, and symbolism as an interconnected whole. This journey led me to develop methods that I believe fall under the umbrella of *linguistic forensics*: the investigative study of language patterns in a text to uncover hidden meanings, connections, and the author's underlying intentions. Through this method, hidden patterns and deeper truths embedded in the text begin to emerge.

In this book, this approach is used to identify distinct terms within the Genesis narratives, delve into their original meanings, and trace their usage outside the allegories. By doing so, we can gain insight into the author's deeper intentions and how these terms were meant to be understood within the allegories themselves.

In essence, linguistic forensics allows us to peer into the author's mind, providing a well-informed estimation of the stories or events they may have contemplated when crafting the creation and Fall narratives. This process uncovers hidden symbolism and clarifies the intended message of the text. However, this is not a simple task—it requires a deep understanding of the original language to identify words that carry nuances that alternate word choices may not convey.

In fact, there are approximately twenty such Hebrew words—terms that carry distinct nuances in their usage outside the allegories. These meanings cannot be ignored when we encounter the same words within the allegories themselves. Together, they reveal an extraordinary depth of symbolism hidden within these narratives. I use the term "hidden" deliberately because, for us, living thousands of years removed from the original language and cultural context, much of this symbolism remains obscured. Yet, to ancient Jewish readers, many of these layers of meaning would have been readily apparent, illuminating dimensions of the text that often elude modern readers.

In exploring linguistic patterns, I discovered they align with the ancient Jewish interpretive framework, offering an established interpretive method.

Rediscovering Gezerah Shavah

I was intrigued when I first noticed this pattern—only to discover later that Rabbi Ishmael had formalized it nearly two thousand years ago in his *Thirteen Principles of Torah Exegesis*. One of his principles mirrors my approach by linking shared language to uncover deeper meaning. This technique, called *gezerah shavah* (גזירה שוה, geh-zee-RAH shah-VAH), connects verses based on shared words or phrases to reveal linked meanings. Encountering this principle felt profoundly logical to me.

To pique interest and demonstrate this interpretive technique, let's preview one such word, *badal* (בדל, bah-DAHL), which is used on days one, two, and four of creation to describe the "dividing" of light from darkness, the waters above from the waters below, and the dry land from the surrounding seas, respectively. Outside the allegories, this word is used exclusively to refer to separating the clean from the unclean, the holy from the profane, and the separation of Israel from the surrounding nations.

By applying this nuanced understanding of *badal* to its use within the creation allegories, we can see that the days of creation are about far more than the separation of physical phenomena; they emphasize the separation of the sacred from the secular. What these holy and profane elements of creation represent will be explored as we progress through this book.

A Fresh Perspective

All of this calls for a fresh perspective. When one revisits these distinct Hebrew terms, their deeper meanings begin to reveal the mysteries woven into the first three stories of Genesis. This approach, rooted in linguistic forensics, demonstrates the connections discussed earlier and highlights their significance in the allegories.

In addition to the linguistic forensics methods already outlined, we must also draw on the insights of St. Gregory of Nyssa. His classic work, *The Life of Moses*, inspires an insightful approach to interpreting Scripture—one that is essential for anyone seeking to understand the Bible through an Eastern Orthodox spiritual mindset. St. Gregory's method complements and enriches our interpretive framework, providing a guide for uncovering the depth embedded in the text.

In St. Gregory of Nyssa's Footsteps

St. Gregory's interpretive framework complements the allegorical depth revealed by methods like *gezerah shavah*, offering a spiritual lens through which to view the text. This model treats each story not just as history but also as a guide for the soul. Every Christian would agree that our task is to conform ourselves to Christ's image. Therefore, every story naturally reveals the tragic consequences of following the path of chaos and sin, contrasted with the blessings of walking a path that leads to order, obedience, and ultimately stillness—a state of inner peace and communion with God, central to Eastern Orthodox spirituality.

As the reader might observe, I employ a hybrid method that combines elements from Jewish and Eastern Orthodox interpretive traditions. Like St. Jerome, to whom I have dedicated this book, I appreciate the significance of maintaining insights rooted in the original language and cultural context. Put another way, while I draw from Jewish interpretive methods, the dogma and tradition of Eastern Orthodoxy serve as the north star guiding my efforts, ensuring alignment with the faith's spiritual and theological foundations.

Painting a New Picture

As you engage with the ideas presented herein, I invite you to embrace a valuable lesson imparted to me by a teacher many years ago. This lesson is relevant to how I hope you will interact with the presented material, for it can serve as a beneficial approach to all aspects of life. The insight I'm referring to was shared at a workshop I attended in the early 1990s. This advice profoundly impacted me and has remained a guiding principle for over thirty years. I frequently recall it in any learning environment.

Letting Go of Preconceptions

To paraphrase the advice given to us that day, mentally pack up all your "I knows" and leave them at the door. You cannot perceive a truth contrary to held beliefs if, with every point made, you immediately raise an objection. Doing so prevents a new picture from being painted in your mind by the words and ideas presented.

There is a well-known story in Zen Buddhism about a professor who visits a Zen master:

> A university professor went to see Zen Master Nan-in to inquire about the path. While serving tea, Nan-in kept pouring it into the professor's cup until it overflowed. When the professor pointed this out, Nan-in replied, "You are like this cup, full of your own opinions and speculations. How can I show you Zen unless you first empty your cup?"

Seeing the Whole Picture

To view things anew, we must avoid seeing them in bits and pieces, starts and stops. We must suspend all disbelief while this new knowledge is being presented and experienced. Only once we have fully opened ourselves in this way can we decide which view makes the most sense. Regardless of the conclusion that we reach, this process ultimately enriches our understanding of the topic at hand.

Unlike a jigsaw puzzle, I cannot show you a picture of the box cover to illustrate how the pieces fit together. Instead, the pieces must be slowly assembled before your eyes. Once that is done, you can decide if they make more sense in this new arrangement.

Likewise, painting a picture to show the viewer the image you have in mind cannot be a collaborative process. The viewer must sit back and wait until the picture is complete. Constant interruptions, such as saying, "I think a tree should go here or a cloud there," would prevent the painter from conveying his vision.

Author's Note

This book includes an optional chapter, "Scriptura but Not Sola," that explores the relationship between Scripture and tradition in depth. While it is particularly designed for readers who embrace the principle of Sola Scriptura, the chapter offers valuable insights that complement the main themes of the book. Whether or not you hold this perspective, you may find it helpful in broadening your understanding of these foundational concepts.

If you choose to read this chapter, you may encounter some repetition of ideas in later sections. This is intentional and serves to reinforce key concepts while maintaining continuity for readers who skip the optional material. Those who prefer a more streamlined journey through the book can bypass this chapter without losing the core message. However, be aware that this chapter includes unique content that is not presented elsewhere.

Whether you read the optional chapter or continue directly into the main text, this book is designed to guide you on a transformative exploration of Scripture's deeper truths.

Part One

Foundation for Understanding

We begin by exploring the creation and Fall narratives of Genesis, seeking their meaning through a closer examination of these ancient texts. By immersing ourselves in the worldview of the ancient Near East and engaging with the language, literary structures, and cultural context, we can approach these passages with a fresh perspective, challenging modern assumptions and uncovering their depth.

Rather than treating these stories as mere historical accounts or cosmological explanations, we will explore them as allegories conveying timeless spiritual truths. From the creation of the "heavens and earth" to both the creation and fall of man, these narratives go beyond recounting beginnings, offering insights into humanity's relationship with God, the nature of creation, and the challenge of aligning ourselves with divine purpose.

These chapters introduce interpretive tools rooted in the cultural and theological context of the original audience, illuminating the symbolic depth of these texts. As their meanings emerge, we will see their relevance not as relics of the past but as living stories for today.

This approach neither reduces Genesis to abstract metaphors nor oversimplifies its lessons. Instead, it reveals how these narratives form the foundation of God's plan for humanity, serving as guides with enduring wisdom and spiritual insight for the journey of faith.

Chapter One

The Three Genesis Narratives

The Creation of Sky and Land

Imagine standing beneath the vast expanse of the ancient Near Eastern sky, where the heavens appear as a shimmering dome arched above a land stretching to the distant horizon and resting on the mountains. For the ancient Hebrew people, this was their universe—their "sky and land."

To understand the Genesis narratives, we must step into their worldview, setting aside modern assumptions. These stories do not address the mechanics of the universe's creation, which lay entirely outside their considerations. Instead, they convey spiritual truths about God's relationship with humanity, the nature of creation, and the journey of aligning our lives with divine purpose. Rooted in the Hebrew text and the ancient Near Eastern understanding of geography and cosmology, they offer not a scientific explanation but a symbolic depiction of divine order emerging from chaos, filled with timeless insights for our spiritual journey.

The first of the three Genesis narratives that we will explore is *The Creation of Sky and Land* (Genesis 1:1–2:3). By reexamining the language and cultural context of this text, we uncover its spiritual depth, challenging conventional translations of key Hebrew terms and viewing the narrative as an allegory that reveals God's purpose for mankind.

To better understand this perspective, let's briefly consider the ancient Near Eastern understanding of geography and cosmology, which shaped their view of creation.

Geography

The ancient Hebrew people did not understand the earth as a planet in geographical terms. Instead, they viewed it as the known land, which ranged from Egypt and possibly parts of Nubia in the south to the territories of the Hittites (now modern Turkey) and the Aegean Sea in the north. To the east, their perspective extended to the Arabian Peninsula and Mesopotamia. These areas constituted the "four corners of the earth" in the conceptions of both authors and readers of that era, reflecting a worldview that was limited yet gradually expanding.

Cosmology

With respect to cosmology, the ancient Hebrew view of the universe was shared by many in the ancient Near East. The heavens were seen as a solid dome, referred to as the "firmament" in the first Genesis narrative, and it rested on the distant mountains. Above this dome were both the dwelling place of God and the "waters above," which would fall as rain through openings in the dome. The sun, moon, and stars were set ***within*** the dome, moving across the sky as part of the ordered structure of creation.

For these reasons, given today's vastly broader understanding of the "heavens and the earth," most readers wrongly conclude that the Creation story is about the creation of the universe. As such, it seems highly misleading to translate the Hebrew words *shamayim* (שמים, shah-MAH-yeem) and *eretz* (ארץ, EH-rehts) as "heaven and earth," respectively. Instead, they are most accurately rendered as "sky and land"—specifically, within the geographical region mentioned above.

The Creation of Man

I will refer to the second creation story, found in Genesis 2:4–25, as *The Creation of Man*. I use "Man" deliberately, in its collective sense, to reflect the creation of humanity as a whole. This narrative begins with the nation of Israel, which is described as a "man in our image," emphasizing the collective identity over the individual creation of a single man and woman. Both creation accounts reflect God's preparation to establish a people in His image by granting them His presence and the Law. While this interpretation may seem surprising to some, I believe that as we explore further, it will become clear that this is the most logical understanding of the text.

This understanding of humanity's creation sets the stage for the next narrative, which explores the consequences of humanity's failure to live in harmony with divine purpose.

The Fall of Man

Beyond the two creation stories mentioned, we have *The Fall of Man*, found in Genesis 3:1–24. This story teaches us the most about the silent path, for in understanding how the Fall came about, we are also given the way back to God. It is my view that *The Parable of Balaam* provides us with much of the story's imagery, with supporting narratives, which we will unveil as we move forward, contributing to the lessons it seeks to convey.

Rooted in historical interactions between God and His chosen people, these narratives gain deeper meaning when viewed allegorically. As we progress, we will explore texts such as *The Song of Moses* and *The Parable of Balaam*, in chapters bearing the same names, that shed light on recurring themes and reveal the symbolic depth of the Genesis accounts.

Viewing the Narratives as Allegories

In the two chapters mentioned above, we will explore the themes of creation and the Fall, which encapsulate the historical cycles of the nation of Israel within a few concise allegories. When viewed through an allegorical lens, these narratives effectively convey complex, recurring themes through their characters, events, and settings. While reflecting a specific period in Israel's history, they also offer timeless lessons about the cyclical relationship between the Israelites and God. These lessons extend to every individual's relationship with God, as the Law of Moses is ultimately fulfilled and recapitulated in the gospel of Jesus Christ.

By "allegories," I refer to narratives that use characters and events to convey deeper spiritual truths rather than strictly literal historical accounts. For some readers, this perspective may challenge traditional interpretations; however, it opens the door to a deeper understanding of Genesis's spiritual depth. Viewing these stories as allegories allows us to explore their broader significance without negating the possibility of concurrent historical interpretations—a viewpoint supported by scholars such as Dr. John H. Walton.[1]

Viewing the Narratives in Their Original Context

To fully appreciate the Genesis narratives, we must engage deeply with their historical, linguistic, and cultural roots. By examining the Hebrew text within the framework of the ancient Jewish worldview, we uncover the layers of meaning and recurring themes often overlooked in modern readings. Tradition complements this textual study, offering a vital guide that ensures

---

[1] *Dr. John H. Walton*, an Old Testament scholar and professor emeritus at Wheaton College, specializes in ancient Near Eastern contexts of the Bible. His works, such as The Lost World of Genesis One, focus on interpreting Genesis through its original cultural and theological framework.

our interpretations align with the spiritual purpose of these narratives. This integrated approach—grounded in the original languages, enriched by Jewish perspectives, and guided by tradition—provides a holistic means of engaging with these ancient allegories.

As we have seen, understanding Genesis requires stepping into the ancient worldview, embracing its cultural and linguistic context, and viewing its narratives as allegories that transcend time. This approach allows us to see the depth of Scripture—not as isolated historical accounts but as living stories woven into the fabric of history, tradition, and divine purpose.

However, this approach to engaging with Scripture prompts a larger question: How do we ensure our interpretations align with the intended messages of the author(s)? To explore this, we must consider the relationship between Scripture and tradition, recognizing that while Scripture is divinely inspired, it flourishes within the context of tradition. This invites us to reflect on how passed-down wisdom complements personal engagement with the Scriptures, ensuring a faithful understanding.

Chapter Two

Scriptura but Not Sola

This chapter addresses two distinct audiences: readers who hold to *Sola Scriptura*—the belief that Scripture alone is the sole authority for Christian faith—and Eastern Orthodox Christians seeking tools for dialogue with such proponents. While this discussion is not directly tied to the book's primary focus of deepening our understanding of Genesis, it provides a valuable framework for understanding how tradition and Scripture work together to preserve Christian truth.

Since this holistic approach is foundational to how this book presents its material, I invite readers to explore the complementary nature of tradition and Scripture, as explained in this chapter. Conversely, those who are acquainted with and receptive to the role of tradition in interpreting Genesis might view it as optional.

Tradition's Complementary Role

Tradition does not replace Scripture but serves as a guiding framework to ensure our interpretations align with its spiritual objectives. To fully appreciate the depth of Genesis—and all of Scripture—it is essential to recognize the indispensable role tradition plays in enriching our understanding and pointing us toward the ultimate truths these texts convey.

To effectively address the Sola Scriptura position, we must first dismantle the idea of a "great apostasy," for it is the cornerstone of its proponents' arguments.

The Great Apostasy Myth

Proponents of Sola Scriptura often justify their approach by appealing to the concept of a "great apostasy," claiming the Church abandoned true doctrine at some point in history. However, this idea lacks substantial historical evidence. Moreover, those of us who reject the notion of a great apostasy are not responsible for disproving it, as proving a negative is inherently impossible. Instead, the burden of proof lies with those who assert that such an apostasy did indeed take place.

In their efforts to demonstrate this event, various extraneous doctrines are often cited as evidence of the alleged apostasy. Yet, these were explicitly denounced by early Ecumenical Councils and synods, which steadfastly preserved apostolic teachings. One such heresy is *Montanism*, which arose in the mid-second century and emphasized the necessity of ongoing revelation through prophetic utterances, ecstatic visions, and speaking in tongues. Often regarded as an ancient precursor to modern Pentecostalism, Montanism was condemned by multiple synods, including those in Asia Minor and Rome, as the Church affirmed the sufficiency of Scripture and apostolic tradition over claims of new revelation.

Christ Himself warned that "an evil and adulterous generation seeks after a sign"[2]—a caution against the spiritual dangers of prioritizing external displays over the inner work of humility and purification. Those who seek public demonstrations of self-confirming signs risk being diverted from the transformative path of repentance and communion with God.

Ironically, many heretical ideas cited by proponents of the "great apostasy" theory align more closely with Sola Scriptura advocates than with the councils they reject. These advocates often portray such heresies as representative of "original Christianity,"

---

[2] Matthew 12:39

likely because they resonate with their own theological positions rather than the historical faith preserved by the Church. However, rather than validating their claims, this only underscores how heretical ideas, like persistent weeds, repeatedly resurface in the garden of the Christian faith, regardless of how often they are uprooted.

Four Foundational Flaws of Sola Scriptura

Sola Scriptura suffers from four fatal flaws that are manifest in their proponents' logic.

1. The New Testament epistles, which form the foundation of faith for Sola Scriptura proponents, are merely appendices.
2. Proponents misunderstand the message in 2 Timothy 3:16-17.
3. The Scriptures themselves advocate that believers should be taught in the apostolic tradition by one who has received the passed-down vision.
4. All Scripture is taken out of context if it is not understood within the framework of ancient tradition.

Flaw 1: The Epistles are Appendices

Scripture, particularly the epistles, was never intended to serve as a standalone theological manual. The New Testament epistles were written as context-specific letters addressing the needs and disputes of early Christian communities. These communities received the gospel primarily through the oral teachings and lived examples of the apostles. This oral and lived tradition formed the "book" of their faith, with the epistles functioning as corrective appendices to this larger narrative.

What we know for certain is that the apostles never taught the Church to be solely reliant on Scripture as the foundation of their faith. An examination of a couple of key passages from St. Paul confirms this.

Flaw 2: Misunderstanding St. Paul's View

A key verse often cited in defense of Sola Scriptura can be found in 2 Timothy:

2 Timothy 3:16–17

16 Every Scripture is God-breathed, and profitable for teaching, for reproof, for correction, and for instruction in righteousness,

17 so that the man of God may be fully qualified, completely equipped for every good work.

While this passage affirms Scripture's divine inspiration and immense value, it does not imply that Scripture alone is sufficient. The historical and theological context of this letter presupposes a community of faith guided by apostolic teaching and oral tradition. Furthermore, Paul was primarily referring to the Hebrew Scriptures—the Law (*Torah*), the Prophets (*Nevi'im*), and the Writings (*Ketuvim*)—since the New Testament canon had not yet been formalized.

Although Paul's letters were recognized as authoritative in some early Christian communities, it is unlikely that he, out of basic humility, intended for his writings to be considered part of "Every Scripture." Yet, Sola Scriptura advocates often cite this passage to justify a heavy reliance on Paul's epistles, even though he was likely referring to the Hebrew Bible—the Scriptures of his time.

We must also view this passage from 2 Timothy alongside his counsel to the Thessalonians:

2 Thessalonians 2:15

15 And so, brethren, stand firm and keep the traditions which we taught you, whether by word or by letter.

Here, Paul explicitly instructs Christians to adhere to both the oral traditions delivered in person and the written teachings found in his letters. This highlights that apostolic tradition, in both its oral and written forms, was essential to the early Church's faith and practice.

Flaw 3: Being Untaught in the Apostolic Tradition

Peter confirms the necessity of being taught how to read and understand the Scriptures when he acknowledges the complexity of Paul's writings:

2 Peter 3:16

16 He does so in all his letters, speaking of these things. However, his letters contain some things that are hard to understand, which the untaught and unstable twist to their own destruction, as they also do with the other Scriptures.

These passages collectively point to a biblical truth: understanding Scripture requires proper teaching, mentorship, and illumination. This is further illustrated when Philip encounters the Ethiopian eunuch reading Isaiah. When asked if he understands the text, the eunuch replies, "How can I unless someone guides me?"[3]

Similarly, the disciples, who spent years with Jesus, failed to comprehend the Scriptures until after His resurrection. On the road

---

[3] Acts 8:30–31

to Emmaus, Jesus "explained to them what was said in all the Scriptures concerning Himself."[4] Later, to an even larger group of disciples gathered in Jerusalem, "He opened their minds so they could understand the Scriptures."[5]

These examples consistently demonstrate that Scripture was never intended to stand alone. It was entrusted to the apostles and their successors, who conveyed its meaning through teaching and tradition. Without this framework, Scripture remains a sealed mystery, subject to misinterpretation by those untaught in the apostolic vision.

Flaw 4: Out of Context

Overemphasizing isolated Scripture passages underscores the need for tradition, which is rooted in the interpretation of the Church's living faith. Scripture warriors often like to accuse their opponents of taking a verse out of context when it doesn't agree with their own views. Still, every verse is taken out of context when it lacks the broader view provided by a two-millennia-old tradition. Tradition provides the continuity and communal understanding needed to preserve the transformative power of God's Word, guiding believers toward communion with Him.

The Unbroken Promise of the Church

Trying to assemble a puzzle without the full picture leads to the aimless shuffling of pieces—and relying solely on human reasoning is no different. Whether we are rearranging Scripture verses or fragments of human philosophy in a search for meaning, both approaches are fundamentally flawed. This mirrors Eve's sin: instead of trusting the divine instruction passed down through Adam, she relied on her own imperfect reasoning to discern right

---

[4] Luke 24:27

[5] Luke 24:45

from wrong, elevating herself as the ultimate authority. Likewise, proponents of Sola Scriptura reject any intermediary—any "Adam"—between themselves and God, asserting personal authority to determine doctrinal truth but risking the same error of subjective and unguided judgment.

This approach also reflects a lack of trust in the unbroken tradition that Christ promised would endure: "and the gates of Hades will not prevail against it."[6] To suggest that the Church fundamentally abandoned Christ's teachings challenges this promise. If we trust in Christ's faithfulness, how can we reconcile the idea that "true Christianity" disappeared for over a millennium? Such a view is not only inconsistent but also undermines the very assurance that Christ gave to His followers.

Doctrinal Accuracy vs. Inner Transformation

We must carefully evaluate the implications of focusing solely on "doctrinal correctness tradition," particularly when compared to the Eastern Orthodox approach, which emphasizes the transmission of a communal understanding and living examples alongside accurate doctrine.

While doctrinal accuracy is vital as a guidepost for the Christian life, it alone does not guarantee entry into the inner kingdom of heaven. True transformation requires embodying Christ-like qualities such as humility, love, forgiveness, and obedience to God. Doctrine must be complemented by a tradition that provides tangible examples of how to live out these truths in meaningful and transformative ways.

Barriers to Transformation

Unfortunately, misunderstandings about Christ's nature often arise in traditions that lack this holistic approach. Without the

---

[6] Matthew 16:18

continuity of an unbroken tradition, efforts to "reimagine" Christ frequently result in distorted portrayals. In popular culture, for instance, Christ is sometimes depicted as a detached mystic delivering abstract aphorisms or as an emotionally unstable figure consumed by His circumstances. Such portrayals fail to convey the fullness of His teachings, His perfect obedience to the Father, and His embodiment of dispassion—a serene equanimity that reflects divine love and purpose.

This fragmentation extends beyond doctrinal disputes to our very conception of God. Without the framework of tradition to guide us, many people inevitably project their understanding of authority figures, particularly their earthly fathers, onto God. For some, this may lead to seeing God as overly harsh or distant, while others may imagine Him as permissive or detached. Tradition safeguards against such projections, providing a clear and communal understanding of God as revealed through Christ, who perfectly reflects the Father's nature.

How Tradition Supports Our Transformation

The Eastern Orthodox tradition emphasizes Christ as the perfect God-man—fully divine and fully human—who reconciles heaven and earth through His life, death, and resurrection. This understanding is not merely theoretical but is made tangible through the lives of the saints and the Church's communal life. The Church is often described as a "hospital of the soul," where believers find healing and restoration through prayer, sacraments, and fellowship. In this context, Christ is not viewed as an offended deity waiting to condemn humanity but as the loving Savior who seeks to restore us to communion with Him.

In some interpretations, the idea of an offended deity stems from attempts to reconstruct Christianity using Sola Scriptura, often divorced from the living tradition and communal understanding that reveal God's love. When Scripture is read in isolation, it can lead to a distorted perception of God's nature and intent.

To guard against this, our Lord has given us the saints—living examples throughout history who embody the mind and attributes of Christ. Through their lives, we witness how God's love is manifested and how He truly is. As Christ stated, "Whoever has seen me has seen the Father."[7] If this could only be said of Christ, humanity would have no living examples to follow. Thus, He ensured not only the faithful transmission of His teachings but also the ongoing witness of lives transformed into His image.

Practical Transformation Exemplified Through the Saints

The Orthodox tradition brings this witness to life through its saints, such as St. Mary of Egypt, St. Augustine of Hippo, and St. Moses the Hungarian. These saints exemplify inner transformation and the pursuit of divine communion. Their struggles and victories illuminate the path of repentance, showing us how to embody the virtues of humility, prayer, and love. The Church preserves this path to healing, providing the faithful with essential tools and guidance to attain salvation and eternal communion with God.

Orthodoxy corrects overly intellectualized and emotionally distorted interpretations of Christ's nature, transmitting both doctrinal truth and the living witness of those transformed by it. Through this synergy, Christ is understood as He truly is: the Son of God who entered creation to restore humanity and lead us back to communion with Him.

The Inherent Quandary of Sola Scriptura

Sacred tradition is indispensable on this journey of transformation. It enables us to progress from chaos to order, from darkness to light, and ultimately into union with God. These

---

[7] John 14:9

traditions, embodied in the sacraments and the Divine Liturgy, are not mere symbols but active means of grace. They prepare our hearts and minds for illumination, allowing Scripture to truly transform us.

Without this preparation, efforts to interpret Scripture risk being led by human reasoning rather than the Spirit of God. Tradition ensures that we follow the biblical pattern of purification, illumination, and union, thus enabling us to fulfill our purpose and be made in God's image.

The reader should appreciate the inherent quandary: without purification preceding illumination, there can be no correct understanding of Scripture. At the same time, without tradition, there is no established path of purification and no living example to which we can conform our lives to achieve an illuminated mind. This interdependence of purification and tradition reveals the inadequacy of Sola Scriptura as the foundation of faith, for it neglects the essential framework that enables the Scriptures to accomplish their divinely intended purpose in our lives.

By embracing both Scripture and tradition, we unlock the deeper truths of Genesis and all of Scripture, allowing God's Word to illuminate not only the ancient world but also our spiritual journey today. These truths converge in the Torah's overarching theme. By exploring its message, we gain insight into the Genesis allegories and the unity of the entire Bible.

Chapter Three

The Timeless Torah

We have outlined the scope of the three allegories in this work and considered the significance of Scripture—not as a stand-alone authority but as one interpreted within the framework of tradition. This tradition emphasizes Scripture's overarching message, providing the necessary context for understanding its deeper intent.

Within this framework, the Torah—the first five books of the Bible, known as "the Law"—takes on a central role. Far from being a mere collection of commandments, rules, and rituals, it serves as a guide for spiritual transformation, ultimately pointing to Christ. Without grasping the Torah's primary message, we cannot fully appreciate the significance of *The Song of Moses* and *The Parable of Balaam* or the truths they inspired within the creation and Fall narratives.

While traditional Jewish understanding holds that "the way" is encapsulated in the oral and written Law, Christ revealed its fullest expression by embodying a life fully aligned with it. To grasp the message of the Torah, we must consider Christ's teachings and how He lived it.

The Beginning of the Way

Many perceive the teachings of Moses and Christ as fundamentally different, revealing a significant disconnect between how Christians today view the Torah and how Christ understood it.

Since Christ taught from the Old Testament, it follows that profound spiritual truths are embedded within it—truths that have often been overlooked. Christ illuminated aspects of its teachings that others failed to recognize, showing that the Christian journey is present within the Torah when approached with the correct spiritual perspective.

For the Law's message to find its fulfillment in Christ's teachings, Moses must have held the proper spiritual mindset. In his time, this meant grasping the deeper purpose of what was revealed to him on Mount Sinai—not simply to establish external rituals but to direct the hearts and minds of the people of Israel toward inner transformation.

Despite Moses's efforts, this spiritual mindset did not become an enduring, shared perspective within the nation. This limitation highlights the difficulty of moving from external observance to the inner transformation that the Law was always meant to inspire—a transformation in which "man" becomes a "man in our image."

Losing Our Way

The transmission of spiritual truths through Moses to the children of Israel reveals a recurring pattern: when profound teachings are entrusted to those who lack spiritual insight, they are often misunderstood. Instead of being recognized as tools for inner transformation, these teachings are reduced to external rituals and practices—forms more accessible to the spiritually blind but merely hint at their deeper meaning.

As generations pass, the absence of the original lawgiver leaves the people without the necessary spiritual guidance to preserve the teaching's true essence. Though the words and rituals may be faithfully maintained, the spirit behind them begins to fade. Yet even in this diminished form, the teachings retain the potential to be life-altering for those who are open to transformation.

The Wisdom and Pitfalls of Rituals

This dual nature of rituals—their power and their vulnerability—illustrates both their wisdom and their pitfalls. Rituals serve as a bridge, engaging the body in preparation for the mind to grasp truths it cannot yet comprehend. Over time, participation in these practices can awaken the deeper spiritual insights they contain. However, the majority may never fully understand the Law's purpose, and still, in every age, there are those who transcend mere observance and are transformed by its divine intent.

When Leadership Fails

However, most adopt a mindset wherein the community's activities become merely a cultural experience while, for others, it devolves into rigid legalism. Unfortunately, the next generation of leaders is often drawn from these two groups. As such, institutions that once protected these truths end up in the hands of those motivated more by power and authority than by spiritual maturity.

These leaders often mistake external markers—honorifics, accolades, and positions of authority—for signs of spiritual growth. Their sense of progress is measured by human praise rather than God's approval. Such leaders' lack of spiritual depth is often exposed when, through one circumstance or another, they lose or fail to obtain a desired leadership position or suffer an embarrassing setback; they fall away because their roots lack depth.

St. John Climacus, in *The Ladder of Divine Ascent* (1982), warns against this in step 22:

> A vainglorious man is a believer—and an idolator. Apparently honoring God, he actually is out to please not God but men
> . . .
> The servant of vainglory leads a double life. To outward appearance, he lives with monks; but in his heart of hearts he is in the world.

> . . .
>
> The Lord often humbles the vainglorious by causing some dishonor to befall them.

The humble, focused on inner change, avoid positions of power, leaving room for the self-serving to dominate. Over time, these individuals cause the living tradition to fossilize. They leave behind a distorted understanding of the original teachings, mingling them with their own self-important interpretations and man-made laws.

Christ's Rebuke of Legalism

It was in this condition that Christ found the faith He had established centuries before as the great "I AM." He sharply rebuked some of the religious leaders of His time—calling them "whitewashed tombs which appear beautiful on the outside but are full of dead bones inside."[8] In this condemnation, He exposed their tragic descent into legalism and hypocrisy.

The metaphor of tombs is particularly fitting, as one of the gravest sins a spiritual leader can commit is imposing man-made rules that divert followers from the transformative path of God's true teachings and the deeper purpose of rituals. Instead of guiding the people toward the inner battlefield necessary to reestablish the Garden of Eden within their hearts, these leaders shepherd them to spiritual death by turning their focus outward—toward pleasing man rather than God.

The Burden on Followers

Followers caught in this web find themselves trapped in a dual struggle: striving to please earthly leaders while attempting to reconcile the divine Law with the laws of men. This creates a

---

[8] Matthew 23:27

Gordian Knot of spiritual confusion that feels impossible to untangle. It raises a profound question: how can one honor tradition and respect spiritual leaders while also discerning and setting aside their human impositions on divine revelation?

This dilemma places the worshiper in an uncomfortable position, akin to that of Eve—selectively dismissing parts of what is handed down while accepting the rest. It reduces faith to a piecemeal approach, turning people into "cafeteria Christians." Such a predicament undermines the ultimate goal of eliminating chaos to establish inner tranquility, leaving followers mired in confusion rather than advancing toward spiritual transformation. For this reason, I refer to the creation and passing down of man-made rules as the absolute worst thing a spiritual leader can do.

The Need for Discernment

This conflict epitomizes the core challenge faced by those seeking to follow the true path amidst a landscape of distorted teachings. It highlights the critical need for discernment and the courage to question established norms when they deviate from the essence of God's instructions.

Unfortunately, the types prone to curry the favor of such leaders are often those groomed to become the next generation of leaders. Born into religious traditions, they may conform outwardly but lack the personal transformation that comes from a genuine encounter with God. For them, religion often becomes a cultural institution focused on status, praise, and recognition rather than spiritual growth. Even for the spiritually minded, these temptations are often close at hand. We see this exemplified in Christ's own disciples.

Lessons from Christ's Disciples

Christians tend to read the New Testament stories and place the Scribes and Pharisees at one end of the spiritual spectrum and

Christ's disciples at the other end. However, the disciples were not immune to misunderstanding the Law or seeking personal gain. Some sought positions of honor, asking to sit at His right and left hand in His kingdom. They failed to grasp that He had come to establish an inner, spiritual kingdom—not an earthly one.

This misunderstanding reflects how far the Israelites had strayed from a proper view of the Scriptures, for even the twelve chosen from the nation struggled to perceive their true meaning.

Rediscovering the Way

Yet even as the children of Israel strayed from the Law's transformative purpose, Christ's life and teachings revealed the way back. This revelation marks the beginning of rediscovering the path, which requires embracing the Torah's deeper spiritual meaning. Let us explore how Christ illuminated this forgotten way.

Christ discerned that the Torah's deeper purpose was not to be a rigid set of commands or a system of sacrifices but was designed to bring about the inner transformation that He later articulated in the gospel. In this sense, the beginning and culmination of the Law share the same ultimate goals—to bring humanity into alignment with God's will and encourage lives of spiritual renewal.

In the Gospel of Luke, our Lord declared, "The kingdom of God is within you."[9] His message, and the message of the Law from which He taught, centered on transforming a chaotic world into one of divine order, enabling humanity to enter this inner kingdom. If we fail to see this transformative purpose within the Torah, then we fail to understand it as it was intended—as Christ Himself understood it.

In Eastern Orthodox tradition, the process of turning chaos into order is known as the hesychastic path. This term, which I

---

[9] Luke 17:21

previously introduced, derives from the Greek word *hesychia* (*ἡσυχία*, EE-see-CHEE-ah), meaning stillness or quiet. Stillness is the prerequisite for knowing God, as the psalmist declares, "Be still, and know that I am God."[10] This path involves a process of purification—a cleansing of the mind and heart from the distractions and passions that darken the eye of the soul.

Christ affirms this connection between purity and spiritual vision when He says, "Blessed are the pure in heart, for they shall see God."[11] This hesychastic path is more than an Eastern Orthodox practice; it is the thread running through the entire Bible. It embodies the transformative journey intended by the Torah's teachings and later fulfilled in Christ's life. Scripture's allegories repeatedly point to this path, urging us to embrace purification and stillness as the means to restore divine order within.

Moses, the original lawgiver, introduced humanity to this way of transformation. Christ, in turn, exemplified it through His life and teachings, revealing the inner kingdom as the ultimate destination of this journey. In the chapters ahead, we will examine how *The Song of Moses* and *The Parable of Balaam* illuminate this path. These foundational texts offer key insights into the creation and Fall narratives about God's plan for humanity—insights long obscured to so many readers due to its rich symbolism grounded in a required understanding of the Hebrew language and cultural context.

---

[10] Psalm 46:10

[11] Matthew 5:8

Part Two

The Allegories' Inspiration

As we delve deeper into the Genesis narratives, it becomes clear that their imagery and message are intricately connected to other passages in the Torah, whose overarching message—expressed through its stories and teachings—charts a transformative path. As we've already seen, they are designed to show mankind the path of purification that leads to spiritual renewal.

In the chapters ahead, we will explore two foundational passages from the Torah: *The Song of Moses* and *The Parable of Balaam*. Although distinct from the creation and Fall narratives, these texts hold the key to unlocking their allegorical meaning. By applying interpretive techniques such as inclusios and linguistic patterns, we will reveal convincingly tight connections between these passages and the initial Genesis narratives, shedding light on the deeper truths they convey.

Chapter Four

The Song of Moses

Inclusios: The Hidden Key to the Allegories

To uncover the major themes of Genesis and the Bible's overarching purpose, it's helpful to explore interpretive tools that illuminate hidden connections. One such tool is the *dis legomenon* (*δίς λεγόμενον*, THEES le-GOH-meh-nohn), which refers to a word that occurs only twice within a text or corpus. Another is the "inclusio," a literary structure that frames a passage using repeated words or phrases, linking its sections into a unified whole.

Though distinct, both concepts rely on repetition to draw attention to key ideas. In this discussion, we'll focus on the inclusio as a framing device. The inclusios we will explore are limited to those whose "bookends" involve *dis legomena*. In other words, the bookends are marked by a shared word that appears only twice in the named text. These tools reveal strong connections between *The Song of Moses* and the creation allegories, offering new insights into the biblical narrative. This approach falls under what I've termed *linguistic forensics*—a method for uncovering hidden literary patterns and their theological significance.

To demonstrate how inclusios work, we'll begin with a relatively simple example from the Gospel of John. In one chapter, a single term frames the passage, creating a cohesive structure and uncovering layers of meaning within a concise section. This example sets the stage for exploring larger-scale inclusios that span the biblical narrative, from Genesis to Deuteronomy.

Illustrating the Power of the Inclusio

In the Gospel of John, our Lord says, "In my Father's house are many mansions."[12] In this verse, the Greek word for "mansions" is *monē* (*μονή*, moh-NEE), a term that appears only twice in the entire New Testament—both occurrences within this single chapter. The second appearance of this term is in verse 23:

> **John 14:23**
>
> 23 Jesus answered him, "The one who loves me will keep my word; my Father will love him and we shall come to him and make ***a home*** in him."

In this context, "a home" comes from *monēn* (*μονὴν*, moh-NEEN), a variation of *monē* that we encountered in verse 2. Both verses—one at the beginning and another near the end of Jesus's dialogue—employ the same term, creating a cohesive structure that links two aspects of a unified idea: God's dwelling resides within the believer. This connection might have been clearer to English readers if the translators had consistently rendered both occurrences of the Greek term with the same English equivalent.

Spiritual Mansions: Building the Kingdom Within

The "mansions" mentioned by Jesus are not literal structures in a distant heaven but symbolic representations of God's presence within us. In the Gospel of Luke, our Lord says, "The Kingdom of God does not come with observation"[13] and "The kingdom of God is within you."[14] If the kingdom resides within, then our heavenly "mansion" must also be found inside of us. Preparing for God's

---

[12] John 14:2

[13] Luke 17:20

[14] Luke 17:21

indwelling involves aligning ourselves with His teachings and building a spiritual "mansion" that reflects the purification and illumination brought about by His grace. This is why there are "many mansions"—each unique to the relationship we cultivate with God.

This metaphor of spiritual mansions frames our understanding of inner transformation, much like inclusios frame key biblical themes. Inclusios serve as literary "bookends" that link passages together, revealing deeper connections and emphasizing essential truths. Having explored the metaphor of mansions, we now turn to the dual inclusios that tightly connect *The Song of Moses* with *The Creation of Sky and Land* allegory, demonstrating how these texts illuminate each other's meanings.

Dual Inclusios in the Creation Narratives

Returning to *The Song of Moses*, we find not one, but two inclusios that tie this Song to the Creation allegory. These literary markers emphasize the connection between these key passages, underscoring the deeper spiritual truths they convey.

Inclusios are powerful tools that draw our attention to the cohesiveness of entire passages, allowing us to delve more deeply into the themes highlighted by each half of the inclusio. They remind us that the Bible is not a random collection of stories but a unified narrative, intentionally crafted to reveal God's plan through allegory, symbolism, and spiritual insight. By recognizing these patterns, we uncover a divine coherence that shows how each part of Scripture is carefully structured to bring us closer to understanding God's vision for humanity.

Having explored how inclusios can emphasize meaning within a single chapter, we now turn to examples that extend across entire books of the Bible. Here, two inclusios bridge *The Song of Moses* and *The Creation of Sky and Land* narrative—not just across verses or chapters but across all five books of the Law. These literary markers reveal deeper connections between creation and communion with God, illustrating the continuity of God's purpose from the beginning.

Inclusio 1: Tohu, a Wasteland

The Hebrew word *tohu* (תֹּהוּ, TOH-hoo) carries a range of meanings: "emptiness," "waste," "desert," "chaos," and "confusion." One significant instance of this term is found in *The Song of Moses*:

Deuteronomy 32:10

10 He found him in a desert land, and in the ***waste***, a howling wilderness; He compassed him about, He cared for him, He kept him as the apple of His eye.

The other half of this inclusio is found in *The Creation of Sky and Land* allegory:

Genesis 1:2

2 Now the earth was ***unformed*** and void, and darkness was upon the face of the deep; and the spirit of God hovered over the face of the waters.

In these two passages, *tohu* is translated as "waste" and "unformed," respectively. Both instances of *tohu* serve as bookends, framing the narrative structure that spans from Genesis 1:2 through Deuteronomy 32:10. This inclusio ties the Creation allegory to *The Song of Moses*, suggesting that the journey of Jacob mirrors the transformation depicted in Genesis—from a state of disarray and confusion to divine care and order.

Each occurrence informs the other, framing the intervening text and shaping it into a cohesive narrative. The choice of *tohu* is not arbitrary; it carries a specific weight and meaning that ties the two ends of the Torah together. They not only inform each other's meaning but illustrate that the entire intervening text of the Torah is about the transformation of moving from both a physical and spiritual chaotic wilderness to an ordered Promised Land.

There are several Hebrew terms for wilderness or wasteland, such as *charbah* (חרבה, khah-reh-BAH) and *midbar* (מדבר, meed-BAHR). The latter is the most frequently used, appearing 105 times throughout the Law. By contrast, *tohu* is used only twice. This rarity suggests that the author(s) selected it intentionally due to its nuance. Unlike the other choices, which primarily refer to physical desolation, *tohu* also conveys a sense of confusion and disorder—an essential element in the allegory of creation.

When an author chooses a rare word over more common synonyms, it's worth asking why. In this case, the additional connotation of confusion in *tohu* enriches our understanding of these passages, highlighting the movement from disarray to divine order. This nuance is crucial to grasping the depth that the author(s) intended to convey in the allegory. If we truly believe the Bible, in its original language, was divinely inspired, then we cannot think words were casually selected—as if any synonym would suffice.

Inclusio 2: Rakhaf, Hovering Over

To further emphasize the unique connection between these two passages, we encounter a second inclusio—the Hebrew word *rakhaf* (רחף, rah-KHAHF), most commonly translated as "hover over." This rare word, found only in *The Song of Moses* and in Genesis 1:2, creates yet another set of bookends that link these seemingly disparate passages. The dual linkage makes coincidence a highly unlikely explanation for this occurrence. It suggests that the author(s) intended to create a strong and deliberate connection between the beginning and end of the Torah. The author(s) wanted to make the conclusion unavoidable that *The Song of Moses* was the inspiration behind the Creation allegory.

This illustration highlights the tight binding between the two passages through a dual inclusio.

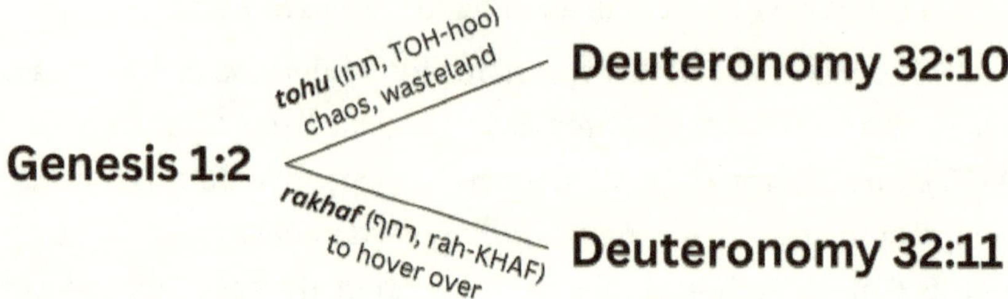

Dual Inclusios: Possible Explanations

The rarity of *tohu* and *rakhaf* within the Torah suggests deliberate significance. These terms appear only in *The Song of Moses* and the Creation narrative, opening up several possibilities.

Intentional Breadcrumbs by the Author(s)

One explanation is that the author(s) of the Torah intentionally linked *The Song of Moses* back to the Creation story. In this view, these terms serve as subtle "breadcrumbs," guiding readers to connect the message of the Song to the symbolism of the allegory. This interpretation aligns with the oral culture of the ancient people of Israel, where memorization and thematic connections were central to understanding Scripture.

Natural Thematic Overlap

Another possibility is that both passages were written in close temporal proximity, leading to a natural thematic overlap. If the same author composed both passages, the recurring vocabulary might reflect subconscious patterns of thought rather than deliberate linkage.

There is also the possibility of thematic overlap, even if the allegories were written much later by authors other than Moses. This possibility exists under the "Documentary Hypothesis," also known as JEDP, which suggests that the Torah was compiled from four main sources: the Jahwist, Elohist, Deuteronomist, and Priestly sources. The author(s) of the Creation narrative may have been influenced by the terminology of *The Song of Moses* as one of the final passages of the Torah, subtly weaving its phrasing and themes into the allegory's text.

God-inspired Breadcrumbs

In my view, these terms are more likely "breadcrumbs" inspired by the Spirit of God. They subtly reveal the foundational stories the author(s) had in mind as they shaped these narratives allegorically. This guidance may have been subconscious, reflecting the interplay between divine inspiration and human authorship.

An Undeniable Connection

Regardless of the explanation, the use of these rare words is unlikely to be coincidental. Together, *tohu* and *rakhaf* link two defining moments in the Torah: the creation of the world from chaos and God's guidance of His people through the wilderness, delivering them from the darkness of Egypt to Mount Sinai, where they would receive the Law—a guide to transforming their own darkness into light. This repetition invites readers to consider the profound connections between creation, chaos, and divine care—foundational themes that thread through the entire biblical narrative.

Inclusios serve as structural markers that frame and unify key passages, revealing connections that might otherwise be overlooked. In the case of *The Song of Moses* and the Creation narrative, the inclusios created by the rare words *tohu* (waste, chaos) and *rakhaf* (hover over) tightly link these texts, demonstrating that the message of the Song is embedded within the allegory's symbolism and themes. This deliberate connection suggests a lens through which we can interpret the allegory, revealing deeper truths about divine order, redemption, and humanity's spiritual journey.

Similar Imagery

The connection between the Creation allegory and *The Song of Moses* runs deeper than the inclusios of *tohu* and *rakhaf.* These distinct words serve as structural markers, but they are just the beginning of a more intricate relationship. Both texts explore God's transformative power, moving from chaos to order and shaping the world according to His divine will.

The Song of Moses reflects on God's interaction with the Israelites, recounting how He brought order to the wilderness of Jacob's condition. Similarly, the Creation allegory depicts the transformation of formlessness into a structured world, presenting God as the ultimate creator of life and purpose. These parallels encourage us to consider *The Song of Moses* as a lens through which we can interpret the allegory, revealing its deeper symbolism and theological truths.

The remainder of this chapter explores the shared themes and imagery between these two texts, focusing on their use of water, the heavens and earth, and divine teaching. By examining these connections, we uncover a unified message about God's creative and redemptive work, offering a glimpse into the Torah's theological coherence.

Addressing Heaven and Earth

Moses begins his song by summoning both heaven and earth to bear witness to his words, a powerful invocation that echoes the opening of Genesis:

Deuteronomy 32:1

1 Give ear, ye heavens, and I will speak, and let the earth hear the words of my mouth.

Genesis 1:1

1 In the beginning God created the heaven and the earth.

The Genesis 1 narrative continues with each aspect of heaven and earth addressed individually: ". . . and God said . . ."

Genesis 1:3-24

3 Let there be light

6 Let there be a firmament

9 Let the waters under the heaven be gathered together

11 Let the earth put forth grass, herb-yielding seed, and fruit-tree bearing fruit after its kind

14 Let there be lights in the firmament

20 Let the waters swarm with swarms of living creatures

24 Let the earth bring forth the living creature after its kind

The parallel is striking. In the Creation narrative, God's words bring light, separation, and purpose, turning chaos into order. Likewise, in Moses's song, the recounting of God's deeds reminds us how He brought order and structure to a nation in turmoil. In both cases, heaven and earth are called to witness the words and works of God, linking creation and redemption.

Redemption, after all, is a creative act, as the transformation from chaos to order ultimately shapes a new being—one fashioned in the image of God. Notably, the invocation of heaven and earth aligns with the scriptural principle that "at the mouth of two witnesses,"[15] every matter is established.

Having established the parallels between heaven and earth as witnesses, we now turn to the imagery of moisture and grass, exploring how these elements deepen our understanding of humanity's relationship with divine sustenance.

The Grass of the Field

Before delving into the imagery of moisture, it is important to reflect on its recipient—grass, a biblical metaphor for humanity. This recurring image captures both its fragility and fleeting nature:

Psalm 103:15

15 As for man, his days are as grass; as a flower of the field, so he flourisheth.

Isaiah 37:27

27 Therefore their inhabitants were of small power, they were dismayed and confounded; they were as the grass of the field.

Some may interpret the grass in these passages not as a direct metaphor for mankind but as a symbol of life's fragility. However, the two concepts are intertwined. If an author seeks to convey the brevity and frailty of man, what more fitting image than grass or the flowers of the field, which flourish briefly and then fade?

---

[15] Deuteronomy 19:15

This exploration of grass as a metaphor will lay the groundwork for a deeper discussion of biblical plant imagery in the upcoming chapter, "Herbs and Weeds as Types of Humanity," where we will examine how these symbols reflect humanity's spiritual journey.

Moistening the Earth

Verse 2 of the Song tells us that his teaching will fall as rain from the heavens upon the entire earth, distilling as dew. This implicitly means that it will be impossible for any person on earth to walk anywhere without being touched by it:

Deuteronomy 32:2

2 My doctrine shall drop as the rain, my speech shall distill as the dew; as the small rain upon the tender grass, and as the showers upon the herb.

This imagery resonates with the Creation narrative in Genesis:

Genesis 2:6

6 but there went up a mist from the earth, and watered the whole face of the ground.

Both texts present a picture of the earth being moistened, one from above and the other from below. In *The Song of Moses*, this metaphor illustrates how God had already formed and shaped Jacob by setting him apart from all other nations. Through the revealed Law and, more importantly, through God's presence, Jacob was distinguished from the rest of the world.

The rain from God's presence is like a nourishing downpour that touches every part of the land. Just as rain, in the Song, brings life to every blade of grass, God's teaching, as it transforms from the Law to the gospel of Jesus Christ, eventually spreads over all the earth.

The "moistening" imagery in both the Song and the Creation narrative presents a deliberate contrast, each symbolizing a unique form of nourishment. In *The Song of Moses*, which reflects a time when God had already given humanity the Law as a means to be transformed into His image, it is symbolized as rain that descends from the waters above as a sign of God's life-giving presence, intended to enliven the spirit.

Genesis, however, describes a time before man was created in God's image. Mist rises from the chaotic waters below, symbolizing humanity's initial state—a condition marked by limited spiritual sustenance. This underscores the need for divine intervention to transform and elevate humanity beyond this primal state.

This contrast accentuates the spiritual depth of the rain in *The Song of Moses*, suggesting a divine form of nourishment. We will now explore how the symbolism of rain and mist conveys distinct and profound messages, uniquely enriching each narrative and often overlooked in traditional readings.

Moistening through Rain

In *The Song of Moses*, rain is used as a metaphor for God's teachings, as expressed through the *leqakh* (לֶקַח, LEH-kakh), meaning "doctrine" or "instruction." Moses describes this doctrine as rainfall, signifying not only God's presence but also the divine wisdom he received and passed down to the children of Israel.

Rain, in this context, is more than just a metaphor for spiritual teaching—it represents the very breath of life, transforming humanity from a mere existence into beings made in the image of God. This idea aligns with the ancient Near Eastern cosmological model, wherein God's dwelling was envisioned above the earth, beyond a dome that separated the heavens from the land.

Rain, falling through openings in this dome, was seen as a physical blessing from God, nourishing the earth and allowing life to flourish. Thus, rain becomes a symbol of God's grace, of his teachings descending from above to nurture the soul.

The word for rain, *matar* (מטר, mah-TAHR), appears thirty-eight times as a noun and seventeen times as a verb throughout the Hebrew Scriptures, consistently portraying it as a divine gift. It is associated with God's teachings because both come from above.

In turn, the teaching is associated with the giving of life, just as rain gives life to the earth. This link between God's word and the granting of life is affirmed in the teachings of Jesus. After delivering a sermon in the synagogue of Capernaum, Jesus addressed His disciples, saying as follows:

John 6:63

63 It is the spirit who gives life; the flesh profits nothing. The words that I speak to you are spirit, and [they] are life.

Just as Moses received the Law and passed it to the children of Israel, giving them life and purpose, so too does Christ's teaching breathe spiritual life into humanity. Through both the Law and the Presence, God breathed life into Jacob, lifting him from the state of a man ruled by dark, beastly passions to one who embodies divine order and righteousness.

God's gift of life through His teachings has extended beyond Israel to all nations. The rain of His word has fallen across the entire earth, and no corner of creation has been left untouched by its grace. Like rain settling on every blade of grass, God's teachings have spread across the world, nourishing all who are willing to receive them.

Moistening through Mist

In *The Creation of Man* narrative, we encounter the metaphor of moistening the earth just before the creation of a "man in our image." This detail invites us to pause and ask: if the account is taken as literal history, why was it necessary to moisten the "whole face of the ground" before forming man? If moisture were needed to create clay for man's formation, as the literalist would have us believe, only a small portion of the ground would have required it.

Such questions arise whenever allegory is treated as literal history because the sequence of events often seems illogical or out of place. In an allegory, however, every element holds symbolic meaning that points to deeper truths.

Consider the nature of the mist that arises in Genesis 2:6. The moisture comes from below—the chaotic waters of the earth. Mist or ground fog is the result of evaporation from lakes, rivers, oceans, and even soil moisture. As such, the mist represents the nurturing of life from the very chaotic waters from which it was drawn. It is only transformed through the evaporation process.

Contrasting Rain and Mist

In the process of evaporation of the waters below, they are purified as contaminants are removed. Once purified and having ascended, this water is no longer ordinary; it has become holy, ready to descend as a blessing upon mankind. In this context, the separation of waters above from waters below becomes a symbol of the distinction between the holy and the profane, the clean and the unclean. The unclean can only become clean and holy through the removal of all that pollutes it from below. It reflects the transformation of chaos into order, which is a shared key theme in both the creation narratives and *The Song of Moses*.

The mist in *The Creation of Man* narrative stands in stark contrast to the rain described in *The Song of Moses*. Here, Moses speaks of rain—or divine teaching—that descends directly from God's presence, symbolizing revelation given to a people already set apart and entrusted with the Law. In Genesis, however, the mist represents an earlier time, before Israel had been distinguished from the surrounding nations and received the Law at Mount Sinai.

Without God's Law, humanity relied solely on natural reasoning and human wisdom for guidance. The mist, therefore, serves as a symbol of incomplete nourishment, insufficient when compared to the divine rain of God-given instruction. Like the waters below, humanity can only become pure and holy by shedding worldly contaminants and ascending into the presence of God.

Understanding the symbolism of water in this way allows us to see how *The Creation of Man* allegory is not merely about the literal formation of man but about God's shaping of His chosen people. Just as water is purified through evaporation, so too is the nation of Israel purified through its journey from chaos to order, from bondage to freedom. The mist represents the early stages of their formation, while the rain represents the full revelation of God's Law.

In this light, the creation of "man" in Genesis serves as an allegory for God's formation of Jacob, the first nation to be taken from the earth and empowered to conform to His image.

The Symbolic Meaning of the Waters Above and Below

In *The Song of Moses*, the teaching of the Law is compared to rain falling upon tender grass. This imagery inherently asks us to consider a symbolic interpretation: from where did the Law, or the teaching, descend? The answer is from atop Mount Sinai. Thus, it is reasonable to interpret the "waters above" as symbolically representing the heights of Mount Sinai. In contrast, the "waters below" correspond to the chaotic waters amidst which the children of Israel dwelt. To these heights, Moses ascended to receive the Law, which then descended like rain to nourish and bring life to the people below.

When Moses descended from Mount Sinai, he brought with him two essential elements of this life-giving rain: the written Law and the divine guidance and instruction entrusted to him, which illuminated the Law's purpose and application for the people of Israel. Without both the written Law and this spiritual illumination, the people would have remained in darkness. This dual transmission finds further affirmation in Solomon's wisdom, where he underscores the necessity of both vision and obedience for spiritual growth:

Proverbs 29:18

18 Where there is no vision, the people
perish: but he that keepeth the law,
happy is he. (KJV)

This verse highlights the importance of both divine vision to illuminate the purpose of the Law and obedience to the Law to provide structure and direction. On multiple occasions, Solomon equates the Torah with life itself.[16] On one of those occasions, he writes, "Keep my commandments and live, and my law as the apple of thine eye."[17] In this instance, "my law" is translated from the Hebrew word *torati* (תורתי, toh-RAH-tee), emphasizing the Torah's central role as divine teaching that sustains and directs life. Solomon contrasts the life-giving power of divine instruction with the

---

[16] Proverbs 3:1–2; 6:23; 13:14

[17] Proverbs 7:2

destructive path of temptation, reinforcing the Torah as both a safeguard and a source of wisdom.

With this understanding, rain descending to water the ground symbolizes the granting of spiritual life through the deliverance of both the Law and God's presence, preparing humanity to receive and nurture divine life. This reading reveals the creation narratives as more than a description of physical acts; it portrays the divine process of transforming chaos into life-giving order through both the written Law and the vision of its purpose.

By understanding the "waters above" and "waters below" in this way, we see unity between the giving of the Law at Sinai and the Creation story. Both illustrate the same divine act: God's Word and Spirit descending to transform chaos into order and bring purpose, life, and renewal to humanity.

Chapter Five

The Parable of Balaam

Plains of Moab

In *The Song of Moses*, shortly after comparing his doctrine to rain that falls and nourishes the earth, Moses speaks of how God divided the nations and chose one group as His people and inheritance. This historical event, I argue, serves as the basis for the second allegory in Genesis, *The Creation of Man*, in which God takes one man, Jacob, from all the nations, breathes the breath of life into him, and thereby makes him in His image.

In his song, Moses writes how God found Jacob in a "waste," *tohu*, of a wilderness and cared for him:

Deuteronomy 32:10

10 He found him in a desert land, and in the waste, a howling wilderness; He compassed him about, He cared for him, He kept him as the apple of His eye.

This moment in *The Song of Moses* unlocks the deeper meaning behind the creation allegories in Genesis. The connection extends to other stories in the Torah, such as when the Israelites lived in the plains of Moab, which the prophet Balaam described as "gardens by the river-side."[18] However, they fell into the forbidden

---

[18] Numbers 24:6

sin of idolatry with the daughters of Moab. This parallel between Israel's encampment in the plains of Moab and the Garden of Eden narrative reveals how each location serves as both a place of divine provision and a test of faithfulness.

The Plains of Moab: Eden's Inspiration

The experiences of Israel in the plains of Moab parallel the lessons of the Eden narrative. In Moab, Jacob's descendants lived in a kind of paradise where God provided for them, similar to the Garden of Eden in *The Creation of Man* narrative. In both settings, however, the people succumbed to temptation—the men of Israel with the daughters of Moab, as well as Adam and Eve with the forbidden fruit.

Eventually, the Israelites were commanded to leave this life of ease, where God had provided manna, to cross the Jordan, conquer the land, and earn their sustenance in the same way in which Adam and Eve were commanded to earn theirs: 'by the sweat of their brow.' The parallels are unmistakable.

The wilderness, often viewed as barren and uninhabited, was transformed by God into a garden for Jacob, just as He created the Garden of Eden for Adam and Eve. This transformation culminated during Israel's final encampment in Moab at the end of their forty-year journey, where Balaam poetically observed:

Numbers 24:5–7

5 How goodly are thy tents, O Jacob, thy dwellings, O Israel!

6 As valleys stretched out, as gardens by the river-side; as aloes planted of the Lord, as cedars beside the waters;

7 Water shall flow from his branches, and his seed shall be in many waters; and

his king shall be higher than Agag, and
his kingdom shall be exalted.

Before we explore how this imagery connects to Eden, it is worth examining the symbolic elements Balaam uses. The "dwelling tents of Jacob" in Moab are likened to orderly rows of aloes and cedars, both of which carry deep significance: aloes, known for their fragrance, symbolize healing and spiritual depth, while cedars represent strength and longevity.

These trees are placed by the waters, indicating divine provision and hinting that the fruit from Israel's branches would fall as "seed" and eventually flow into "many waters"—symbolically, to all nations. Balaam understood, however, that the true strength of the nation of Israel was in their God; it was not simply in their territorial expansion but also in the spread of His Law and His presence.

The parallels between Moab and Eden extend further. Both places are depicted as lush with trees, and in both, the inhabitants were provided with food without labor—manna in Moab and fruit-bearing trees in Eden. Additionally, a river flowed outward from both locations, symbolizing the spread of divine blessing to all nations. In this way, the plains of Moab emerge as a significant influence on Eden's imagery, illustrating God's continual provision and His desire for His blessing to reach all corners of the earth.

The Four Rivers: Divine Providence for All Nations

In *The Parable of Balaam*, the waters flow from the branches of Jacob, who are metaphorically referred to as aloes and cedars, to carry its seed to all the world. *The Creation of Man* allegory contains strikingly similar imagery:

Genesis 2:10

10 Now a river flowed out of Eden to
water the garden, and from there it
divided and became four rivers.

At first glance, the connection between these narratives may not be immediately clear. Yet, both convey the same essential message: God's providence, initially granted to Israel, was meant to spread to all nations. This verse in Genesis describes a river flowing through a lush garden filled with trees provided by God. The seeds from these trees would naturally fall into the waters, which then divided into four rivers, carrying the seeds to the ends of the earth.

Though this is not explicitly stated, as it is in *The Song of Moses*, it is implicit that every tree beside a river will benefit from the process of *hydrochory*—a natural process of seed dispersal by water—some seeds settle in distant lands, take root, and grow, representing the spread of God's providence to all humanity.

Real Place Names in Allegory

Many have tried to locate the four rivers of *The Creation of Man* allegory, focusing on the mention of the Tigris and Euphrates—both real, identifiable rivers in the ancient world. This has led some to assume all four rivers are literal, though the Pishon and Gihon remain unknown. Few have considered the reverse: since the Pishon and Gihon may not be real, perhaps all four are allegorical.

It is not uncommon for allegories to include real place names, as we see throughout literature. For example, Dante's *Divine Comedy* uses Florence not merely as a city but as a symbol of political corruption. At the same time, Charles Dickens's *Bleak House* situates its critique of societal injustice in London. Similarly, Victor Hugo's *Les Misérables* employs Paris as a backdrop to explore themes of revolution and redemption. Even in ancient works like Homer's *Iliad*, the Scamander River, now known as the

Karamenderes River in Turkey, serves a symbolic role in grounding mythological events in familiar geography.

The use of real rivers like the Tigris and Euphrates may anchor the Eden narrative in a tangible world. At the same time, the mysterious Pishon and Gihon invite readers to consider their symbolic significance. Together, these elements suggest that Genesis blends the real with the allegorical to convey deeper spiritual truths about humanity's relationship with God and creation.

The takeaway, however, is that the inclusion of real place or river names does not necessarily indicate that the story is intended as literal history. Instead, such names may serve to ground the narrative in familiarity while pointing to larger theological or symbolic themes.

Symbolic Interpretations in Jewish and Christian Thought

Throughout history, many commentators have interpreted the four rivers of Eden symbolically. Philo of Alexandria, in his work *De Opificio Mundi* (*On the Creation of the World*), suggests that they represent the four cardinal virtues: "And they also are four in number, prudence, temperance, courage, and justice." Philo's interpretation of the rivers as virtues underscores their role in nourishing the soul, aligning with the broader theme of Eden as a source of spiritual life and wisdom.

Other early commentators—including the authors of *Targum Pseudo-Jonathan*, Augustine of Hippo, Bernard of Clairvaux, and Thomas Aquinas—also took symbolic approaches, albeit different from Philo's. Some interpretations are more intricate, even overly thought-out.

I prefer the approach in which the authors of Scripture used symbols that are easily recognizable to readers based on a shared language and context without requiring elaborate extrapolations. Following my usual rule of letting the Bible interpret itself, we see that the number "four" in ancient Israelite symbolism often represents order and universality. The "four winds," "four quarters," and "four corners" of the earth signify "everyone and everything." Therefore, the four rivers flowing from Eden could be seen as emphasizing the reach of God's providence, symbolizing the spread of His Law—later exemplified in the teachings of Christ—throughout the entire earth.

This portrayal of rivers flowing out from Eden into the world highlights Eden's role as a unique source of divine blessing. A deeper look at the Hebrew term for Eden itself may provide additional layers of insight into its meaning as a place of abundance and delight, pointing to the fullness of life and blessing intended for all.

Reexamining Eden

I wish to briefly examine the Hebrew word *'eden* (עדן, EY-dehn), which is transliterated in the Scriptures as "Eden." Once again, transliteration has resulted in a loss of nuance, as the term's deeper meanings remain obscured. So, what does *'eden* truly signify?

It is etymologically linked to the Sumerian word *edin*, meaning "plain" or "steppe." This linguistic connection highlights the deep historical roots of the term while suggesting layers of meaning in its use within the Genesis narrative.

This suggests that Eden, often seen as paradise, also carries the idea of it being a "plain," reminiscent of the fertile plains of Moab, which were nourished by seasonal rains and nearby water sources. Balaam poetically described these plains as lush, with trees and gardens by rivers, evoking imagery of abundance similar to Eden. This further supports the theory that the experience of the children of Israel in the plains of Moab inspired much of the imagery in both *The Creation of Man* and *The Fall of Man* allegories.

By exploring the symbolic connections between Moab and Eden, we see that the Genesis allegories are deeply rooted in Israel's historical experience. It illustrates how God's provision and testing shape His people into His image.

Through these parallels, the Eden narrative not only reflects Israel's historical experiences but also reveals God's overarching plan to transform humanity, turning chaos into order and blessing into a means of redemption for all nations.

Part Three

Before and After the Light

At its core, the journey through Scripture is a journey from chaos to order and from darkness to light. These transformative themes are not confined to the opening verses of Genesis but permeate the entire biblical narrative, shaping its message and purpose. In the chapters ahead, we will explore how these polarities—particularly the dynamic between chaos and order—serve as the cornerstone for interpreting the Bible's allegories, parables, and rituals.

Our focus begins with the foundational imagery of light and darkness, often depicted as a *merism*, a rhetorical device that joins opposites to convey a whole. From Genesis to Revelation, the interplay of opposites illustrates the human condition, God's intervention, and the path toward spiritual transformation. The Bible's creation narratives, far from being mere accounts of material origins, unveil the divine process of bringing order to chaos. This process mirrors the hesychastic journey of the soul toward inner stillness and communion with God.

Building upon this foundation, we will delve into the symbolic language of Scripture, examining how key terms and patterns—such as "evening and morning" and "God divided"—convey deeper truths about the boundaries between the sacred and the profane; the clean and the unclean; and ultimately, light and darkness. These motifs not only anchor the creation and Fall narratives but also resonate throughout the Torah, the life of Christ, and the traditions of the Church, offering a cohesive vision of God's work in the world.

As we proceed, these chapters will reveal how the Law, the rituals it prescribes, and the traditions it inspires continue to guide us in our journey from chaos to order. Through this lens, we will see how the Torah and the gospel harmoniously converge, illuminating the transformative path that leads us from the confusion of our natural state to the divine image we are intended to reflect.

Chapter Six

Before the Light

The uncreated light of God's presence permeates the Scriptures, standing in stark contrast to the profound darkness that enveloped humanity for millennia before God revealed Himself.

The Power of Merisms in Biblical Interpretation

The theme of light and darkness permeates Scripture, spanning Genesis, the Psalms, Isaiah, the Gospels, and the Epistles. This duality symbolizes broader concepts such as good and evil, sin and righteousness, and chaos and order—each pivotal to biblical narratives. Among these contrasts, "chaos and order" stand out as uniquely distinct, their definitions largely resistant to evolving interpretations.

Carl Jung explored the interplay of opposites in his book *Psychological Types*, introducing the term "enantiodromia" to describe "the emergence of the unconscious opposite over time." This is a modern expression of what Isaiah perceived thousands of years ago when he declared:

Isaiah 5:20

20 Woe unto them that call evil good, and good evil; that change darkness into light, and light into darkness; that change bitter into sweet, and sweet into bitter!

Isaiah's lament addresses the moral inversion of values, a deliberate and catastrophic act of redefining what is true and good. While enantiodromia highlights the unconscious emergence of opposing tendencies, Isaiah's warning explicitly condemns those who knowingly distort divine order. This inversion mirrors what George Orwell later described in *1984* as "doublethink"—the coexistence of contradictory beliefs that erode clarity and truth.

The Preferred Merism

While many merisms, by their abstract nature, are susceptible to subjective reinterpretation over time, the tension between chaos and order remains distinct. Unlike "light and darkness," which can be diluted into shades of gray, chaos and order resist such equivocation. One either discerns the clear boundaries that establish order, or chaos takes precedence in their absence; there is no middle ground. This clarity emphasizes the lasting relevance of Isaiah's warning, highlighting the fact that disregarding divinely established distinctions leads inevitably to moral and spiritual collapse.

The modern notion of "enlightenment"—celebrated as the ability to perceive everything in shades of gray rather than black and white—is revealed here as a dangerous fallacy. This perspective, rather than signaling wisdom, often becomes a convenient justification for indulging one's own desires and disregarding higher truths. When one sees the world as an indistinct blur of gray, the boundaries between right and wrong, sacred and profane, dissolve, leaving room for the unchecked assertion of self-will over divine order.

This merism of "chaos and order" will serve as a cornerstone in our exploration of biblical themes, particularly in the creation and Fall allegories. I will demonstrate that the Bible's opening is not a narrative about the creation of the universe or a singular man but rather an account of the transformation of chaos into order. This process sets the stage for the ultimate transformation of all humanity.

Creation as a Path to Order

The allegory of *The Creation of Sky and Land* does not overtly reference the previously mentioned polarities. Nevertheless, it effectively communicates these ideas through two significant phrases, "evening and morning" and "God divided," the full depth of which is blurred by the translation process.

Evening and Morning

The original Hebrew text subtly conveys our preferred merism. Each day of creation concludes with the phrase "And there was evening, and there was morning . . .," which effectively underscores this contrast. This repetition emphasizes the structured progression of creation, illustrating how chaos is transformed into a harmonious order.

The Orthodox Jewish physicist Gerald Schroeder wrote the following in his book *The Science of God: The Convergence of Scientific and Biblical Wisdom* (2009):

> The Hebrew word for evening is erev. The root of erev is disorder, mixture, chaos. The Hebrew word for morning is boker, its root being orderly, able to be discerned.

It is interesting to note that the days of creation are reflected in both the Jewish and Eastern Orthodox liturgical days, which start in the evening and continue until the next day when there is light. In the evening, lines are blurred, identities are difficult to make out, and walking without stumbling becomes more challenging. With morning, everything is made clear; we see the boundaries, identities are easy to determine, and the path before us is clear. The liturgical day serves as a reflection of the spiritual journey intended for the worshiper's soul.

As it passes from evening to morning, each day introduces yet another symbol: the emergence of light out of darkness and order out of chaos. Beyond this expression, "and there was evening, and there was morning . . ." another expression operates in tandem to convey the same idea.

And God Divided

The expression ". . . and God divided . . ." appears in the accounts of days one, two, and four, describing the separation of light from darkness, the waters above from the waters below, and day from night, respectively.

There are over a half dozen Hebrew words that can convey the idea of division, but for our purposes, we are only interested in one because it is the word used in the three days of creation just mentioned. It has an exclusive, context-dependent meaning that is quite revealing and helpful in unfolding its intended message within the allegory.

This particular word, *badal* (בדל, bah-DAHL), is found forty times throughout the entire Hebrew Bible, twenty-two of which are found in the Law—seventeen of those being outside this allegory.[19] It is worth exploring these usages to see how the "dividing" or "separating" in the allegory is best understood:

- once in Exodus to speak of the veil that separates the holy of holies
- eight times in Leviticus: twice in describing how to prepare a sacrifice, six times in speaking of separating the sacred from the profane
- three times in Numbers when referring to the separating of Israel from the other nations

---

[19] Exodus 26:33; Leviticus 1:17; 5:8; 10:10; 11:47; 20:24–26; Numbers 8:14; 16:9,21; Deuteronomy 4:41; 10:8; 19:2,7; 29:20

- five times in Deuteronomy: thrice in speaking of separating the cities of refuge, once in setting Levi apart as the priestly tribe, and once for separating evil from the tribes.

I have presented this detailed breakdown for the reader so that it can be easily seen that *badal* is consistently used to speak of separating the sacred from the profane, the clean from the unclean, the holy from the even more holy, and Israel from the rest of the nations. Consequently, it is so exclusive to this particular usage that it can only be concluded that it must carry the same nuance in *The Creation of Sky and Land* allegory as well. Even outside the Law, within the Prophets and Writings, it is also reserved for the same purposes just described. It is never used for any other type of division.

Let's view an example to illustrate how this exclusive, context-dependent application of *badal* is not accidental. Though it is often translated as "divide" or "separate," it is not used in any other cases for an act of separation that is disengaged from the act of distinguishing the sacred from the profane. For instance, it is not used in the dividing of the sea by Moses. Why not? I suggest that this is because earthly waters are metaphors for chaos,[20] and if God divides chaos from chaos, He has not separated the clean from the unclean, nor the sacred from the profane. Therefore, *badal* would be inappropriate in this context.

The Bible's Overarching Theme

These polarities of "chaos and order" are not just the central theme of the creation allegories but also the focus of the entire

---

[20] Water as a symbol of chaos was pervasive in ancient times, extending from Mesopotamian cultures to Canaanite and Ugaritic to Egyptian, Greek, Chinese, Indian, and Hebrew cultures.

Torah. Rabbi Lord Jonathan Sacks, in his book *Covenant and Conversation—Exodus: The Book of Redemption* (2024), referring to Genesis and Exodus, states:

> The overarching theme of both books is the tension between order and chaos. In this, the Torah is not unique. Order and chaos have been the twin polarities of human thought since the birth of civilization, and they remain so today, whether in society or nature. . . . What makes the Torah unique is the way it conceptualizes the two.

I would go further and say the entire Bible repeatedly addresses this tension between opposites. Some might object to this characterization, asserting it is about saving mankind. True! But from what exactly are we being saved? Again, some may respond that we are being saved from death, which arises from sin. However, this raises the fundamental question, "From what does sin arise, if not from the confused state of our thoughts and feelings—a state of mind that arises from a lack of clarity regarding the appropriate distinctions and functions that should exist among various aspects of life?"

Preparing to Move from Chaos to Order

As we enter this world, we all encounter uncertainty about how to navigate life. I compare it to being given a five-thousand-piece jigsaw puzzle without the box's cover and asked to piece together a meaningful picture. Without knowing what the final image should look like, we can't even begin to determine where each piece belongs. This has been the experience of every person since the dawn of time.

We madly seek the missing puzzle box picture that should have been given to us from the start, but it seems there is no way to find it. So many people out there say they have that picture, each looking very different. On the other hand, some look very similar, with only subtle differences. No matter what, we are left with one of two confusing paths: either we aimlessly shuffle the pieces of the puzzle until they hopefully reveal a meaningful picture, or we first undertake the formidable challenge of figuring out who has the right puzzle box picture to help us piece everything together. Both tasks are daunting!

This was how mankind lived for countless millennia before the manifestation of the light that could dispel this darkness. Humanity perpetually floundered in the night, unable to discern order from chaos, with no hope of seeing the dawning light. The task before us today mirrors this ancient struggle, yet with a crucial difference: the divine picture has been revealed, and we can find it if we search.

This revelation marks the transformation from chaos to order, from darkness to light, that we've explored throughout this chapter. Before God revealed this picture, mankind's search was futile, for the image of God remained hidden, and thus, they could not be transformed into His likeness. As we move forward, we'll see how this divine illumination sets the stage for humanity's journey toward reflecting the divine image, guiding us from the confusion of our natural state to the order and clarity of spiritual enlightenment.

Chapter Seven

Let There Be Light

The Burning Bush

Before any image can be painted, there must be light. This was introduced at the burning bush on Mount Sinai when God appeared to a single man, Moses. In essence, this moment is mirrored in the Creation narrative when God said, "Let there be light." The appearance of light at the burning bush was not just a revelation to Moses; it marked the beginning of a transformative journey for all of humanity. This event laid the foundation for God's ongoing work of bringing order out of chaos, a process that would continue through the Law and its guiding light.

This transformative event is allegorized in *The Creation of Sky and Land*:

Genesis 1:3–4

3 And God said, "Let there be light." And there was light.

4 And God saw the light, that it was good; and God divided the light from the darkness.

Following God's revelation to Moses, the unfolding events echoed the separation of light from darkness. God set apart the children of Israel, choosing them from among all nations and granting them a land where they would learn the Law. This Law became the guiding force, teaching them to distinguish clean from unclean, life from death, and the holy from the profane. As they gained awareness of these distinctions, their minds were illumined, and they became a light to others.

This calling is later affirmed in Isaiah, where God declares: "I the Lord have called thee . . . to be a light of the nations."[21] From this perspective, God's leading of Jacob out of the dark wilderness of Egypt can be seen as the historical event that inspired the Creation story's separation of light from darkness. Just as light in creation represents the first step toward divine order, so too does the Exodus and the giving of the Law symbolize the beginning of Israel's role as the bearer of divine light to a chaotic world.

The Law as a Guiding Light

The light was manifest to Moses on Mount Sinai, where God taught him face-to-face. However, the children of Israel were not prepared for such a personal relationship and pleaded with Moses, "Speak to us yourself, and we will listen; but let not God speak to us, or we will die."[22]

As God always does, He met people at their level, giving them an appropriate means to ascend their own metaphorical Mount Sinai, hopefully at some point in the future. The Law served as a lesser form of enlightenment—a guiding light revealing the way out of spiritual darkness.

The Role of the Law: Transformation and Purification

This context explains why, in the Creation allegory, the separation of light from darkness was not simultaneous with the manifestation of light. For the astute reader of the Scriptures, the above passage should prompt this question: Why was there a delay

---

[21] Isaiah 42:6

[22] Exodus 20:19 NASB95

between "Let there be light" and the separation of light from darkness?

The answer lies in understanding that Genesis is not a chronological, historical account of the universe's creation but an allegory. It symbolizes God's act of separating the children of light from the darkness of Egypt and the surrounding lands where idolatry prevailed.

This path was initially revealed to humanity through the Torah, often referred to as simply "the Law," the term that I will use primarily because it is also how the ancient Jews, including Jesus, referred to it. Today, this word causes people to think of a legal code, but in this context, it is really a set of instructions to transform the individual and a nation. A man is transformed only by dispelling the confusion that rules his thoughts and feelings, thus turning his inner world into one that is properly divided and ordered. Only then can peace and stillness prevail.

The Etymology of Torah: Pointing the Way

Since I will refer frequently to the giving of the Law as God's initial teaching to bring man out of chaos, it is worth a quick explanation as to why this is so. HALOT, *The Hebrew and Aramaic Lexicon of the Old Testament* (2000), is the best-known Hebrew lexicon and explains the etymology of the word *Torah*:

> What is probably most likely is a connection with ירה [yah-RAH] in the sense of stretching out the finger, or the hand, to point out a route.

It is no wonder then that Jews would later refer to both the oral and written Law as "the way," *halakhah* (הלכה, hah-lah-KHAH). Similarly, in Eastern Orthodox Christianity, "the way" is understood as the hesychastic path—a journey of purification, illumination, and *theosis*, which is derived from the Greek word *θέωσις* (THEH-oh-sees) and refers to the process of becoming like God. This was

God's intent for mankind from the beginning when He said, "Let us make man in our image." Therefore, *theosis*, for the Christian, can be understood as conforming to the likeness of Christ.[23]

This idea resonates with the original intent of the Law: to guide humanity into a state of holiness. It's important to note that the Jewish "way" and the Eastern Orthodox Christian's hesychastic way are not different. This is what I'm attempting to show the reader—the original Law of Moses has the path of silence intricately woven within its pages. We will see this as we progress through this book.

We often think of the Law as a set of rituals focused on physical purity due to its rules regarding how to deal with the unclean. However, God was never solely concerned with physical purity, apart from its role in preventing the spread of disease. The purpose of external rituals was to condition the mind to think in the same way: clinging to the holy while rejecting the profane. The Christian hesychastic path specifically aims for such a transformation, making the purpose of the rituals much more apparent because we, too, seek to remain separate from all that is unclean within our inner landscape.

Moses's Vision of Christ as the Living Law

The Law by itself turned out to be insufficient to transform mankind. Moses, at the time of the giving of the Law, understood this would be the case. He was not under any misguided notion that the revealing of the Law would solve mankind's plight of being enveloped in confusion. He witnessed firsthand the obstinacy of the children of Israel after the Law was given to them and how that generation had to die out before their descendants could enter the Promised Land. As such, he did not believe that the Law would solve anything in the short term. He knew the illumination of mankind would be a prolonged process, taking thousands of years.

---

[23] Romans 8:29

Knowing this, he gave us two prophecies of One who would show them the way through His life and example:

Numbers 24:17

17 I see him, but not now; I behold him,
but not nigh; there shall step forth a star
out of Jacob, and a scepter shall rise out
of Israel, and shall smite through the
corners of Moab, and break down all
the sons of Seth.

Deuteronomy 18:18

18 I will raise them up a prophet from
among their brethren, like unto thee;
and I will put My words in his mouth,
and he shall speak unto them all that I
shall command him.

Christ as the Missing Picture

Eventually, the new Moses, Jesus Christ, would fulfill these prophecies, showing the way to all of humanity. In the chapter "Before the Light," I wrote of how, before the Law, man's life was like a jigsaw puzzle where the box cover picture was missing. The Law tried to show what that picture should look like, but oral and written instructions were not enough. It required Christ to come and live the Law before our eyes. He essentially supplied the missing puzzle box picture—one that would allow us to vividly see how to assemble the chaotic, strewn pieces of our lives into an orderly, beautiful image in His likeness.

Later, St. Paul would reiterate this same idea to the Galatians:

Galatians 3:24

24 Hence, the law was our tutor which was
to bring us to Christ

What the people failed to grasp from the giving of the Law was later lived out and shown through real-life examples. As such, Christ indeed became the true Way, the true *halakhah*, the full embodiment of the Law lived out perfectly.

I am deliberately tying the Law to "the way" as revealed in Christ's life; otherwise, many will not see how the giving of the Law was indeed the initial step in creating order by separating light from darkness. Christ embodied the Law in a way that serves as the ultimate example for all believers. Yet, only a small number of people were privileged to witness His life firsthand. How, then, could His transformative example be made accessible to humanity across generations?

Tradition as the Continuation of the Living Law

While Christ's life, death, and resurrection are of infinite value in conquering death, this victory would hold limited relevance for our earthly lives if His example could not transcend time and reach each new generation. Spiritual death is overcome not through mere intellectual understanding of doctrines or the historical accounts of the lives of Christ and the apostles but through our transformation into His likeness—a process that demands living examples.

Without the continuous, living image of Christ preserved through tradition, we would rely solely on our imagination to determine how to live the Law as Jesus exemplified it. Tradition offers clarity amidst confusion, equipping us to transform our souls in preparation for eternal life.

This transformation is essential because the soul we cultivate in this life shapes our experience of eternity. We cannot neglect our inner garden, assuming Christ will set it right for us upon His return. Without us learning to tend it ourselves, even after His intervention, it would quickly deteriorate into chaos, overrun by weeds and wild beasts. Christ does not do for us what we must learn to do ourselves. Through the living examples and teachings preserved in tradition, He has given us all we need to become vigilant caretakers of our souls, preparing us for full communion with Him.

God, in His providence, ensured that Christ's image and example would not remain confined to history. Guided by the Holy Spirit, this living example has been faithfully preserved within the sacred tradition and passed down through the Church, offering every generation a clear path to transformation.

The Unbroken Tradition of Living Examples

This legacy lives on not only in the written Scriptures and a shared spiritual mindset but also in the lives of Christ, the apostles, and the saints, as well as the unbroken lineage of bishops. Their actions, teachings, and witness reflect Christ's love, humility, and faith, demonstrating how the Law is fulfilled in a living, tangible way. Through oral, written, and embodied traditions, Christ's life becomes present to us, shaping our journey toward Him.

St. Paul emphasizes this in his letter to the Thessalonians:

2 Thessalonians 2:15

15 And so, brethren, stand firm and keep
the traditions which we taught you,
whether by word or by letter.

This handed-down tradition is not simply a set of teachings but the life and example of Christ Himself—a guide, like the cover image of a puzzle box. Just as a clear image helps us assemble the pieces of a puzzle, tradition provides the clarity needed to reorder our thoughts and align our souls with Him. Without it, we would shuffle the pieces of life aimlessly, hoping to construct something meaningful. Instead, we are called to conform to the image revealed through tradition, allowing it to guide us in the purification of our souls.

Chapter Eight

After the Light

The Deeper Purpose of the Law

Christ's life revealed the deeper purpose of the Law—a framework not only for outward conduct but also for inner transformation. The Law's commandments, rituals, and sacrifices, which implicitly encouraged purity, aimed to shape the soul's ability to discern between clean and unclean, holy and profane. Yet, this purpose had been obscured over time, often becoming more about external compliance than genuine inner change.

Christ made this purpose explicit to His disciples in His teachings. Let's review one example where he teaches the disciples about the deeper meaning of the seventh commandment:

Matthew 5:27–28

27 You have heard that it was said to the ancients, "You shall not commit adultery";

28 But I tell you that anyone who gazes at a woman with a view to lust after her has already committed adultery with her in his heart.

Building Fences Around the Torah

Many Jewish teachers, especially Messianic Jews, interpret Jesus's statement as an example of "building a fence around the Torah," a practice rooted in rabbinic tradition. These "fences," as described in *Pirkei Avot (Chapters of the Fathers)*[24], were intended to prevent inadvertent violations of God's commandments by creating additional safeguards.

For instance, to prevent the unintentional misuse of God's name, the pronunciation of the Tetragrammaton (YHWH, יהוה) was discontinued in public use in ancient times. During Scripture readings and liturgical recitations, other Hebrew words, such as *Adonai* (אדוני, ah-doh-NAI), meaning "Lord," or *HaShem* (השם, hah-SHEM), meaning "The Name," were used in place of YHWH. In more recent times, I have encountered Jewish professors who read the Hebrew letters as "Yod Hey Vav Hey," likely as a modern adaptation to maintain reverence for the sacred name while avoiding its pronunciation. Unfortunately, these practices have resulted in the loss of the original pronunciation and a lack of consensus regarding its reconstruction. For this reason, I have omitted the usual pronunciation guide for this term.

Similarly, Sabbath laws were extended to prohibit even touching items associated with work, such as a pen. Dietary laws were also expanded to forbid mixing meat and dairy, based on the Torah's prohibition against boiling a young goat in its mother's milk. Rabbinic tradition interpreted this command as a broader principle of separation, leading to a prohibition against cooking, eating, or benefiting from mixtures of meat and dairy. This interpretation reflects an emphasis on preserving symbolic boundaries between life-sustaining and life-ending substances.

While these fences aimed to protect the Law, they often became burdensome, shifting the focus from the Law's intent to external adherence. Jesus criticized such practices, saying this:

---

[24] *Pirkei Avot* - authored around 200 CE and includes the oral teachings of rabbinic sages after the Second Temple period.

Matthew 23:4

4 Indeed, they bind heavy burdens that are dreadful to bear and put them on people's shoulders; but they themselves will not lift a finger to help them.

His critique highlights how excessive rules can obscure the Law's original purpose of fostering a relationship with God through inward transformation rather than mere outward adherence.

Clarifying Intent

By emphasizing that the Law's purpose extended beyond outward actions to the inner state of the soul, Jesus was not building additional fences around the Torah but instead clarifying its original intent—to effect inner transformation. He prioritized purity of heart over mere external observance, as illustrated when He said the following:

Matthew 15:17–18

17 Do you not yet understand that whatever goes into the mouth passes into the stomach and then out of the body?

18 But the things which come out of the mouth come from the heart, and they defile the person.

Jesus was not imposing new burdensome laws or implying that the Law of Moses was defective. Instead, He revealed how the Law was always meant to be understood and lived. This understanding highlights the true purpose of the prescribed commandments and rituals—not as ends in themselves but as tools to guide the soul toward inner transformation and alignment with God's will.

But that purpose had long been lost. Over time, as the rules of men outweighed the God-given laws and rituals in their minds and hearts, people became more intent on earning the approval of religious leaders by adhering to these added regulations than on aligning their hearts with God's Law, which aimed for deep, personal transformation. After all, it is far easier to gain the approving smile of a religious leader than it is to engage in the difficult work of inner purification and gain God's affirmation that the inner landscape has been properly tilled and transformed from a wilderness into a garden.

Jesus's teaching on avoiding lust in Matthew 5:28 was less about adding restrictions by putting yet another burdensome fence around the Torah than about revealing the Law's original purpose. The Law centers on purity of heart, not merely purity of physical actions. By making the implicit explicit, Christ clarified that the Law's purpose extended beyond actions to include the inner state, calling His followers to discern righteousness from within.

Although not always stated outright, Jesus's teachings illuminated the purpose and intent of the Law as a pathway to the soul's transformation. This transformation was supported not only by instructions but also by the rituals of the Law, which served as antidotes to inner chaos, guiding the mind and heart into a state of divine order.

Rituals as an Antidote to Chaos

Let's start with a more current example of using rituals to overcome internal chaos. If you're a tennis fan, you will know Rafael Nadal is considered the "King of Clay," having won over sixty clay court titles, including fourteen French Opens. You will also know he has elaborate rituals that he always performs in any match. Two quotes from his memoir *Rafa* (Nadal and Carlin, 2011) explain the value these rituals have for him:

> . . . what I battle hardest to do in a tennis match is to quiet the voices in my head, to shut everything out of my mind but the contest itself, and concentrate every atom of my being on the point I am playing.
>
> . . .
>
> It's a way of placing myself in a match, ordering my surroundings to match the order I seek in my head.

These rituals provide Nadal with a way to stay centered, shut out distracting thoughts, and align his surroundings in a way that might influence his mental focus and order. This effect is not unique to Nadal; rituals are an antidote to chaos for many, offering each of us a way to eliminate distracting thoughts and feelings that otherwise disturb our minds and hearts. By focusing our minds on external actions, we are sometimes able to fill our minds with these activities to the point that unwanted, distracting thoughts cannot find an entrance to the conscious mind.

Interestingly, even simple or "meaningless" rituals can have this effect. For example, Nadal's habit of taking sips of water from two bottles and arranging them in a specific order may seem trivial, yet it quiets his mind. If this alone is all we seek to accomplish through rituals, we don't necessarily need them to have deeper meaning. But rituals can do far more, creating space for internal transformation and order. In the Mosaic Law, we find an application of this principle, where ritual structure serves not only personal order but also establishes boundaries that unite individuals in a shared purpose.

Just as Nadal's rituals help center his mind, the rituals of the Mosaic Law serve a similar purpose—bringing clarity and peace to the Israelites.

The Genius of the Law's Rituals

The rituals of the Law reveal immense wisdom. They structure the mind and heart, establishing clear boundaries and fostering an understanding of purpose. When practiced communally, they unite people and create shared values, defining acceptable and unacceptable behavior. This social harmony addresses a common source of anxiety—the fear of not belonging—and replaces it with a framework of mutual expectations.

Relief from Social Uncertainty

Much of our daily thought revolves around social dynamics: second-guessing conversations and replaying them in our minds to consider how we're perceived. Rituals offer relief from this preoccupation, grounding us in clarity and reducing the cloud of social uncertainty. They delineate boundaries of what is appropriate, a contrast that fades in chaotic or nontraditional societies where individuals set their own rules to gain respect or power. However, this personal pursuit detracts from the deeper purpose of rituals.

True Ritual as Submission

At its core, true ritual requires submission to a higher authority. This submission counters our distracting desire for control, opening inner space for God's presence. To practice spiritual rituals effectively, we must commit fully, setting aside personal desires, opinions, and the need to determine what is right and wrong. Only with wholehearted dedication can transformation unfold. Continuing in doubt or halfhearted effort prolongs confusion, obstructing the clarity we seek.

Avoiding Idolatry

This tension between our will and God's lies at the heart of why Scripture so strongly condemns idolatry: It places the self at the center. Often, we create or adopt gods that reinforce our existing beliefs, demanding minimal change, and thus build barriers to genuine transformation. Timothy Keller, in his book *The Reason for God*, insightfully observes, "If your god never disagrees with you,

you might just be worshiping an idealized version of yourself." We must avoid treating God's teachings like a cafeteria line, choosing only what suits us. True transformation challenges us, requiring us to embrace even the difficult teachings to align more deeply with God's will.

Correction as the Path to Transformation

Some of Scripture's most challenging teachings call us to correct our behavior. To grow spiritually, we must be open to recognizing our faults and understanding that we are not "fine just as we are." Although we may strongly identify with certain desires and tendencies, these do not define us as inherently "good" simply by virtue of being familiar or natural. True growth often requires examining and overcoming even deeply ingrained inclinations. It is delusional to believe that "since I think and feel like this, God must have made me this way." This reflects an inversion, allowing our thoughts, feelings, and reasoning to replace divine truth as the guiding light of our soul.

As such, the darkness within is great. We must embrace correction through the Scriptures and guidance from our church leaders, who are called to model a Christ-centered life. By responding to this correction, we open ourselves to be illuminated from within by the Spirit of God.

In the Book of Job, we find a verse that underscores the importance of accepting correction from God as essential to our peace and well-being:

Job 5:17

17 Behold, happy is the man whom God correcteth; therefore despise not thou the chastening of the Almighty.

We see the consequences of refusing such correction in the lives of the children of Israel, who were liberated from Egypt but remained shackled by a mindset of slavery. They refused to be corrected and were subsequently condemned to perish in the wilderness. A new generation had to rise up, not bound by the same enslaved mindset —a generation whom Joshua could lead into the Promised Land.

No mind tied to the dark habits and mindset of the past can be transformed into one of order. If we are unwilling to let go of our past way of thinking and feeling, no purification or illumination can take place. In like manner, we must eliminate any remnants of idolatry, loyalty to other proverbial gods, and the darkness of our own rebelliousness before we may cross over into the inner Promised Land, thereby regaining the Garden of Eden.

Clearing Inner Space for God

This reorientation of our view of God reveals that He does not demand our worship out of some petty, insecure need for humanity to acknowledge His divinity but to provide us with keys to personal transformation. Worshiping "other gods" or embracing worldly ideologies increases the voices clamoring for our attention. These voices make it harder to "make straight the way before Him"[25] so that He can dwell within.

The goal of worship is not merely to find outer silence but to cultivate an inner space where we hear the voice of the true God within us, uninhibited by external clamor. The goal of our practice is to stop listening to the voices and influences of the world and instead listen to the one and only true God who speaks to us from within.

Not only are the outer voices usually wrong and delay our purification and illumination, but they also prevent the flow of the

---

[25] Isaiah 40:3

river of guidance from reversing its course so that we are illuminated from within. In guiding us toward this silence, the Law's rituals also function as a mode of teaching that deeply engaged both body and soul, embedding its lessons through lived experience.

Teaching Through Ritual and Embodiment

Through the rituals of the Law, there was constant emphasis on the boundaries between life and death, the clean and unclean, the holy and the profane. They provided ways to teach us through movement and action without the necessity of teaching through words.

While rituals and oral teachings are not mutually exclusive, when combined, they are superior because the Law can then be absorbed beyond the conscious intellect. Instead, the teachings are embodied, becoming part of muscle memory, behavior, thoughts, and feelings. It is a way for the disciple to be taught to live the teaching by internalizing it.

This internalization process, so vital to the Mosaic Law, has also evolved within Christian practice, where certain rituals now hold the same purpose of inner transformation without the animal sacrifices of ancient times.

The Evolution of Rituals

Many Christians today tend to view the Law of the Old Testament as something irrelevant—"that was then, but it has no place in Christianity now." However, that is not remotely true. We tend to think that the rituals of those times are meaningless for the modern, sophisticated person.

To understand why Old Testament rituals were central, we must recognize God's intentions behind these practices and the cultural context that shaped them. While animal sacrifice is no longer required, we now participate in the bloodless sacrifice of the Eucharist, which has superseded it.

The Purpose of Old Testament Rituals

A common question among Christians is why God required bloody sacrifices in the Old Testament. It's important to explore this. Of the two culturally endemic practices that the children of Israel brought out of Egypt, God prohibited idol worship while permitting the continuance of animal sacrifices—only redirecting that practice toward worshiping the one true God. This was a transitional practice, weaning away from something that God would later declare He despised.[26]

In the well-known Psalm of Repentance,[27] David reminds us that God's true desire is for a contrite heart; without this, animal sacrifice means nothing. In fact, one could argue that animal sacrifice was allowed so that it could stir contrition in Israelites who were not yet capable of true repentance. This confirms that the Law, with all its rituals, was not designed merely for external obedience but for inner transformation.

The sacrifices were never intended as "get-out-of-jail" cards for sin. The only antidote to sin is to stop sinning, for only in this act do we cease feeling guilt—the very thing that destroys our peace of mind and keeps us from knowing Him.

During the transition to Christian worship, many of these practices took on new forms as the Church adapted these ancient rituals to commemorate and reflect Christ's life and mission. Our focus moved to Him—the final sacrifice for our sins and the ever-living example for our lives.

---

[26] Isaiah 1:11–14

[27] Psalm 51

Transformation through Christian Liturgies

The feasts and festivals of the Old Testament find new expression in Christian liturgies, which invite us to reflect on Christ's life and its transforming significance. Remembering His birth reminds us of light breaking into darkness,[28] a moment echoing creation's first day, when God said, "Let there be light," and separated the light from the darkness.

As we reflect on Christ's selection of His disciples and His teachings to them, we recall God separating Israel's twelve tribes from the nations and calling them a "holy people." This election of the twelve was a reenactment of day four of creation, whose imagery we will explore further in the chapter "Celestial Bodies and Divine Governance."

When we remember His death and resurrection, we find hope in the promise of victory over death through Him. These remembrances parallel the Law's instruction to distinguish life from death.

The distinctions taught through the Law of Moses and preserved in Eastern Orthodox liturgies are now reoriented around Christ, the ultimate High Priest, and the sacrifice for sin. While these rituals have evolved in form, their purpose endures. They integrate Christ's life with the Law and underscore its relevance in guiding believers toward spiritual transformation.

Rituals as Integral to Daily Christian Life

The New Testament, just like the life of our Lord, is in large part a recapitulation of the Law and the life of Moses. Jesus, through His life and teachings, perfectly accomplished what Moses could not do. What the people failed to comprehend through the oral and written transmission of the Law, they were shown by the living

---

[28] Matthew 4:16; Isaiah 9:1

example of our Lord. Through His teachings, by word, deed, and example, the true meaning was conveyed. This is the living Law that has come to us so the light can break forth upon the darkness of our souls.

When the light of Christ illuminated the world and dispelled the darkness, neither He nor His disciples rejected the Law and its rituals. Instead, they remained integral to the daily Christian walk. For Christians today, rejecting or altering the rituals handed down by Christ and His apostles is to deny the very method God has given for internal transformation. These purifying rituals are essential, transforming inner darkness into light and providing a clear path toward illumination and communion with God.

This transformation is gradual—almost imperceptible as night gives way to day. Yet, as we approach dawn, the shift from darkness to light quickens. Until then, we must embody the psalmist's faith:

Psalm 23:4–6

4 Yea, though I walk through the valley of the shadow of death, I will fear no evil, for Thou art with me; Thy rod and Thy staff, they comfort me.

5 Thou preparest a table before me in the presence of mine enemies; Thou hast anointed my head with oil; my cup runneth over.

6 Surely goodness and mercy shall follow me all the days of my life, and I shall dwell in the house of the Lord forever.

Every Christian on this path of purification and illumination walks through this valley of darkness and chaos, trusting that we will reach the other side, where our faith will be rewarded when the house of the Lord comes into sight.

Purity of Heart

Let's consider what all of this is accomplishing for us. As we walk by faith, following the Shepherd through this valley, we learn to release our fears of the unknown. Our thoughts become less troubled by shadows, and over time, this journey acts as a purification process—stripping away thoughts and feelings that obscure a pure heart.

This realization about the importance of a pure heart was pivotal in my conversion to Eastern Orthodoxy. I came to understand that entry into the kingdom of heaven is not about passing a test of doctrinal correctness; if it were, only the intellectually gifted could enter. Reflecting on the endless doctrinal debates of my Protestant years, I began to see their futility—a battle of egos, engaging in countless scriptural sword fights rather than submitting to a higher power. I had been trying to assert what I thought was a superior view of Christianity, treating faith as if it could be reverse-engineered into a "purer" form, assuming it had long ago been lost due to a great apostasy. Such foolishness! In contrast, the Law calls us to a higher consciousness—one that goes beyond intellectual precision and guides us toward an awareness rooted in divine order.

Looking back, I realize that my resistance to Orthodoxy was rooted in an unwillingness to let go of my search for doctrinal precision, a drive born from my experience that, no matter which faith I spent time in, ultimately fell short of presenting a picture of Christianity that was not full of holes. I was like Luther, constructing my own *Ninety-Five Theses*[29] to nail to the doors of all existing Christian faiths, trying to prove myself right—even if mainly in the confines of my own mind. Like so many Protestants and cultists, I

---

[29] *Ninety-Five Theses* was a document nailed by Martin Luther to the door of Wittenberg Castle Church in 1517 as a public challenge to the Catholic Church's practices.

had focused on refining my own faith rather than submitting to the handed-down tradition and dedicating myself to soul purification.

But true doctrinal perfection is beyond us, while the path to purity of heart is open to all. Many of us feel compelled to pursue doctrinal certainty, but this can easily delay our journey toward the perfection that truly matters—purifying the inner kingdom and making a straight path for the Lord. We don't need to complete this process in this life, but we do need to be on this journey, continually drawing closer to Christ, who offers this comforting assurance:

John 6:37

37 All that the Father gives me will come
to me, and the one who is coming to me
I will in no way reject.

Most translations render this phrase as "the one who comes to me . . . ," but this contributes to creating a gross misunderstanding. The Eastern Orthodox Bible provides a more accurate translation: "the one who is coming to me . . ." In other words, it is not coming to Him once, saying some magical prayer of salvation, that allows us to touch home, and we are now safe, as in some children's game of tag. Instead, salvation is an ongoing journey. Those who will be saved are the ones who are in the continual process of coming to Christ, "working out their own salvation with fear and trembling,"[30] and "enduring to the end."[31]

This process isn't about a single moment but about the constant effort to draw closer to Him over time. Only in this way can we hope to have oil left in our trimmed lamps at the coming of our Lord.[32] Those without oil are those who fell down and failed to get

---

[30] Philippians 2:12

[31] Matthew 24:13

[32] Matthew 25:1–13

up again; they gave up on the hope of the prize that lay before us.[33] Christ's promise to not cast out anyone who continually seeks Him is the closest we come to an assurance of salvation: Are we still on the journey, putting one foot in front of the other?

Late in life, I came to see that God calls us to purity of heart and obedience—not merely doctrinal mastery. This purity of heart is essential, for it prepares the way for the inner light of Christ. John the Baptist spoke of this when he urged us to "make straight the way of the Lord." In this verse, John is quoting from Isaiah, where the word "straight" comes from the Hebrew word *yashar* (ישר, yah-SHAHR), which implies becoming "upright" before the Lord.

We are commanded to become like Christ, developing the fruits of the Spirit—love, joy, peace, patience, kindness, goodness, faith, gentleness, and self-control.[34] A true understanding of doctrine will follow naturally as a result of purification and illumination. It is the light within that enlightens the mind; self-reliant thought and reasoning alone cannot fill the soul with anything but darkness.

Through the Church's rituals, we draw closer to becoming like Him. These sacred practices cultivate the purity of heart necessary for genuine transformation, reminding us that it is the reshaping of our inner world that ultimately reflects the image of God.

The Law as a Higher Consciousness

The giving of the Law was, in fact, a bestowal of a higher consciousness—higher than that of what mankind typically experiences and knows as its conscience. Men have always had the latter, but what is it? A conscience is an inner sense of right and wrong, typically formed by our upbringing, societal norms, personal experiences, and adopted beliefs.

---

[33] Philippians 3:14

[34] Galatians 5:22–23

A conscience, however, does not mean we have a structure for sorting out the many inputs we face daily. Everyone has their own unique set of beliefs about right and wrong, and many are hell-bent on convincing everyone else that their set is the right one. There is a large intersection upon which most people can agree. But, no matter how much we might agree, we are still left with a constant inflow of non-authoritative opinions that we must weigh, leaving the human mind in continual doubt as we seek to stumble upon the best set. The Law and the Presence were meant to solve that . . . eventually. Since His set is THE authoritative spiritual mindset we should adhere to, the debate is essentially eliminated, and what is left is to practice conformity to it.

Initially, this was done through external rituals, as prescribed in the Law. These rituals were designed to transform the practitioner's mind, heart, muscle memory, and behaviors. Each individual would be transformed, and since they were being directed to an agreed-upon set of ethics and morality, conflict within and without should also be resolved. They would know what to expect of themselves and others. This is step one in calming the chaos that infects the mind and heart.

Where there is doubt, there can be no stillness of soul. The Law, therefore, prepared the soul for Christ's message, which He would reveal as both a fulfillment and unification of God's enduring guidance.

The Law and Christ: A Unified Message

Much of the Hebrew Bible, after the Law, either points forward to Christ or back to the Law itself. In turn, the Law anticipates Jesus the Messiah. The interconnection between the Law and the life of Christ is unmistakable, each continually pointing to the other. Viewed through this lens, the purpose of Scripture becomes clear: It serves as a constant guide, illuminating God's intentions for humanity's transformation and ultimate communion with Him. They resemble two bookends across the life of Israel, each providing support and meaning to one another, tying all intervening events into a cohesive narrative.

As such, if we do not understand the Law, we cannot understand Christ, nor His life and teachings. Likewise, if we do not understand the life and teachings of Christ, we will miss the point of the Law. We can extrapolate that its themes will continue as a thread throughout the Scriptures, linking everything together.

The True Purpose of Scripture

With this in mind, we have a pretty good picture of what the entire Bible is about. Every passage should be read as though it is trying to teach us about humanity's condition, God's plan to save us, and how we can participate in His plan by engaging in the path He has given to us.

Simple deductive reasoning teaches us that this is what the Bible must be about. Let's follow this trail of reasoning and see why. If we desire to be with God, and stillness is required to know God, then we must eliminate all things that prevent us from experiencing this state of being. Stillness cannot exist as long as chaotic thoughts and desires disturb our minds and hearts continuously. If chaotic thoughts and desires keep us from stillness, then there must be methods by which stillness can be attained. If chaos can be eliminated, and it is ultimately what prevents us from knowing God, then surely the Bible is designed to instruct us in these methods, either directly or through allegories, parables, and metaphors.

When we read the Bible as though it is there to teach us about history, science, or externalities, we can be assured that we are thinking incorrectly about the lessons at hand. St. Gregory of Nyssa, along with other holy fathers, taught us that we should not read the Bible so much as history but as a way to elevate our souls to God.

From Conscience to Higher Consciousness

Reading the Bible in this way and living out its teachings guide us from a normal conscience—an awareness of right and wrong shaped by external standards—to a higher consciousness. This journey takes us beyond a socially agreed–upon morality, reversing the flow so that the world's influence no longer defines our inner world. Instead, our consciousness is shaped by direct communion with God, who clarifies and orders our perception of the world from within.

This inward illumination then shapes how we engage with the outer world, bringing about divine order and deepening our relationship with God. Through this communion, we come to hear His voice and glimpse His uncreated light. This transformation—from a normal conscience to a higher consciousness in communion with God—is what it truly means to be illuminated.

Illumination Requires Entering the Darkness

In conclusion, this series of chapters dealing with the journey from chaos to order, darkness to light, and sin to righteousness is not just the theme of the creation narratives but of the entire biblical message. The separation of light from darkness in Genesis mirrors our own spiritual journey as we walk the hesychastic path, seeking God's light within the darkness of our inner world to find true stillness. We see this reflected in the life of Moses, who had to enter the darkness to encounter God's light.[35]

Just as Moses could have no enlightenment without bravely entering the darkness, there can be no illumination for us if we refuse to penetrate the darkness of our souls and find the radiant light hidden therein.

---

[35] Exodus 20:21

Through the Law, the life of Christ, and the sacred traditions passed down, we are called to a process of inner renewal, in which chaos is dispelled and the divine image is restored. As we continue this journey, may we remember that the purpose of Scripture is not merely to recount historical events but to guide us toward becoming like God, ordering our hearts and minds to know Him fully or as fully as any person is capable of doing.

Part Four

Before a Man in Our Image

We have examined the initial two days of creation, laying the groundwork for the theme of chaos and order while showcasing the allegorical aspects of these stories. Furthermore, we have investigated how this core theme appears in *The Song of Moses* and *The Parable of Balaam,* both inspiring the allegories of the creation and Fall.

The creation narratives in Genesis are more than stories of beginnings—they are allegories, rich with symbolism, that reveal profound truths about humanity, God, and the spiritual journey from chaos to divine order. At their core, these accounts explore patterns of separation and gathering, productivity and barrenness, light and darkness.

Yet when we examine the details—such as the creation of plants, celestial bodies, and living creatures—we encounter narrative tensions that challenge a literal reading. Disparities in timelines, shifts in focus, and unexplained transitions invite us to look deeper. These are not inconsistencies to resolve but invitations to uncover the deeper, symbolic intent of the text.

Each stage of creation unfolds a new dimension of meaning: plants emerge, dry land rises, celestial lights are set in motion, and creatures fill the world—all leading to the creation of humanity, made in God's image. These elements are not just physical; they are spiritual signposts, guiding us to reflect on order, purpose, and transformation.

This journey will move through the days of creation, one chapter at a time. Along the way, we will uncover the spiritual significance of the elements described, revealing how they mirror humanity's calling to grow, bear fruit, and gain dominion—not over the physical world alone, but over the inner landscape of the soul.

Each chapter will explore a new layer of these symbolic foundations, starting with plant life, where the seeds of this spiritual journey first take root.

Chapter Nine

Herbs and Weeds As Types of Humanity

Plant Life in Genesis Allegories

In Genesis, each of the three initial allegories mentions the various kinds of plant life. In the first allegory, which we refer to as *The Creation of Sky and Land*, on the third day, God said, "Let the earth put forth grass, herb-yielding seed, and fruit-tree bearing fruit after its kind." However, in the next narrative dealing with man's creation, after placing him in the Garden, God causes "every tree that is pleasant to the sight, and good for food" to grow out of the ground. Thus, there is an apparent discrepancy between these allegories regarding when plant life was created.

Since I am approaching these stories as allegories, the variations in the timeline are secondary to their symbolic intent; they were never meant to be literal, day-by-day accounts. Despite these differences, each of the three allegories consistently mentions certain categories of plants with symbolic significance, which have been understood throughout the centuries, even down to New Testament times.

With this perspective, we can now explore the symbolism of these plants in a general sense, appreciating how their meanings remain consistent across the allegories in which they appear. Indeed, they are consistent in their symbolic meanings across the entire Bible.

To appreciate the symbolic role of plant life, it is important to first address the challenges posed by a literal interpretation of these narratives.

Questions Raised by Literal Interpretations

Within *The Creation of Man*, Genesis 2:5–6 speaks of something that, on its surface, might seem unimportant as the precursor to the creation of man. However, using *The Song of Moses* as our Rosetta Stone, this passage gives us one of the greatest clues as to the significance of plant life in bearing symbolism that reveals spiritual truths. For this reason, we will review the passage in full:

Genesis 2:5–9

5 No shrub of the field was yet in the earth, and no herb of the field had yet sprung up; for the Lord God had not caused it to rain upon the earth, and there was not a man to till the ground;

6 but there went up a mist from the earth, and watered the whole face of the ground.

7 Then the Lord God formed man of the dust of the ground, and breathed into his nostrils the breath of life; and man became a living soul.

8 And the Lord God planted a garden eastward, in Eden; and there He put the man whom He had formed.

9 And out of the ground made the Lord God to grow every tree that is pleasant to the sight, and good for food; the tree of life also in the midst of the garden, and the tree of the knowledge of good and evil.

Let's consider the host of questions and observations that this passage should raise for those reading the text with discerning eyes. I will only mention a few that occur to me that reveal the inadequacy of a literal reading. They highlight how the text points us beyond surface-level chronology to its deeper symbolic meaning.

Illogical Precursors to Man's Creation: Why does this text begin by discussing elements that have not yet emerged from the earth before it addresses the creation of man? How does the mention of nonexistent plant life provide context for human creation?

The Role of Rain: Why does verse 5 emphasize the lack of rain for plants to grow when verse 6 immediately introduces a mist that watered the entire earth?

Man's Role in Tilling: Why would mankind need to till the ground for plants to thrive when we see plants growing naturally across the world without human intervention?

The Timing of Plant Creation: Another challenge arises from the apparent discrepancy in the creation timeline. In *The Creation of Man*, we are told that God created man, placed him in the garden, and then caused trees "good for food" to grow. Yet in *The Creation of Sky and Land*, Genesis 1:11–13 states that grasses, herbs, and fruit-bearing trees were created on the third day.

The challenges posed by these questions are not problems to be solved so that a literalist viewpoint can be harmonized but invitations to uncover the text's allegorical richness. In these passages, plant life serves as a metaphor for spiritual realities, not as a literal chronology of events. The absence of shrubs and herbs reflects a spiritual condition—an unprepared ground—awaiting humanity's role as cultivator and steward. This imagery indicates a much greater truth that will soon be revealed, but some preparatory groundwork must be laid before that occurs.

Having considered the limitations of a literal approach, we can now explore how plant life serves as a metaphor for humanity, revealing spiritual truths about our relationship with God.

Grass as a Metaphor for Man

In the chapter "The Song of Moses," I briefly mentioned my belief that grass serves as a metaphor for mankind. It is not just grasses and herbs that hold symbolic value but also bushes, thorns, thistles, and trees that hold certain understood references to types of people.

It is essential to acknowledge that these metaphorical values remained significant throughout the millennia of Jewish history. In addition to the Old Testament verses that liken mankind to the grass of the field, Christ also draws similar comparisons:

Matthew 6:28a, 30

28 Consider the lilies of the field, how they grow.

30 But if God clothes the grass of the field which today exists and tomorrow is thrown into the oven, will he not much more clothe you, you of little faith?

The comparison made in these verses is expanded upon in *The Parable of Wheat and Chaff,*[36] where Jesus states that there are two kinds of people: those who belong to Him (the wheat) and those who will be gathered and burned (the chaff).

---

[36] Matthew 13:24–30

Mankind as the Field and Its Workers

Even the disciples did not understand Jesus's parables and came to Him afterward seeking clarification. In verse 38 of the same chapter, our Lord explains to them that "the field is the world." Paul employs a similar metaphor in his letter to the Corinthians:

1 Corinthians 3:9

9 Indeed, we are God's co-workers! You are God's field, God's building.

Notice the similarity between the teachings of Christ and St. Paul in comparison to the creation allegories, where they speak of the different types of plant life springing up. Viewing their teachings in light of the creation narratives would suggest that we are the modern-day man who is charged with cultivating the fields. By mankind representing both the field and its cultivators, it implicitly means that the plants within the field also hold a dual significance.

Symbols of Humanity's Dual Nature Before Adam

There can be no question that grasses, both herbs and weeds, were ingrained in the ancient Jewish mindset as representing humanity. Thus, Genesis 2:5 references two primary types of plants—herbs and shrubs—that symbolize the fruitful and unfruitful. It is a recognition that both types of people existed before God formed a "man of the dust of the ground."

Of course, this runs contrary to the belief that "Adam" was the very first man upon the earth. Such a view prevents the reader from linking the imagery of plant life as symbols of different types of humanity, forcing such a proponent even deeper into a literalist reading of the Genesis narratives.

Having explored grass as a symbol of mankind's transience and dependence on God, we now turn to other categories of plant life that carry equally important spiritual meanings. Each of these plants reveals unique aspects of humanity's spiritual journey.

Shrubs: A Symbol of Desperation and Refuge

We have seen a couple of examples of how the various categories of plants hold specific symbolic value in Jewish society. Let's examine their connotations within the creation and Fall allegories. From *The Fall of Man*, whose verses were just cited, we see two types of plants referenced: *siakh* (שיח, SEE-ahkh), meaning "shrub," and *esev* (עשב, EY-sehv), meaning "herbs," whose symbolic meaning we will explore.

This type of plant, the shrub, is a low-growing woody plant. Plants such as broom, acacia, juniper, and myrtle are commonly found in the Middle East. While humans primarily use these plants for firewood, shade, and medicinal purposes, they have limited value as food. Their utility for animals is greater, as they serve as forage and provide shelter from the sun. Like so many nuanced terms used in the allegories, the selection of these words is not without thoughtful and deliberate consideration.

The Desperation of Hagar and Ishmael

The word *siakh* is only used in two other stories in the entire Hebrew Bible.[37] In both instances, these bushes are a place of refuge for those at the point of death or in otherwise miserable conditions. In the first of these stories, Hagar places Ishmael below one of these bushes to give him a bit of rest in the shade. They have been sent away at Sarah's behest and soon run out of water. Things look dire, and Hagar holds out no hope for the infant's survival.

---

[37] Genesis 21:15; Job 30:4,7

Job Mocked by the Most Pitiful

The same word, *siakh*, is also used in Job 30, verses 4 and 7. At this time, Job has lost everything and is lamenting his pitiful state. He is scorned by the lowest of society's low—people who live among the bushes, extracting from them what meager sustenance they can find. These types of plants serve as food and shelter for the most pitiful and stand in stark contrast to the nurturing value of herbs.

Herbs: A Symbol of Fruitful Servants

Herbs, on the other hand, come from the Hebrew word *esev*. These are non-woody plants and include wheat, barley, dill, coriander, and a host of others. These plants, while also having a purpose for animals, are the primary food sources for man. With this in mind, the contrast between bushes and herbs and their selected use has more meaning for us.

In *The Fall of Man* allegory, we see additional plant life references:

Genesis 3:18

> 18 ***Thorns*** also and ***thistles*** shall it bring forth to thee; and thou shalt eat the ***herb*** of the field.

Here, juxtaposed with herbs, *esev*, we also see thorns, *qotz* (קוץ, KOHTS), and thistles, *dardar* (דרדר, dahr-DAHR). Their imagery is highly meaningful throughout the scriptures, including in the creation and Fall narratives. Therefore, we will spend the greatest amount of time in this chapter to understand their significance.

Thorns and Thistles: A Symbol of the Ungodly

Scripture frequently employs thorns and thistles as vivid metaphors for ungodliness and spiritual hindrance. In 2 Samuel, we read, "But the ungodly, they are as thorns thrust away, all of them."[38] The Hebrew word for thorns, *qotz*, appears twelve times[39] in the Hebrew Bible, while the Hebrew word for thistle, *dardar*, appears only twice.[40]

Interestingly, while "thorns" are sometimes mentioned alone in the Scriptures, "thistles" are always paired with thorns in a noun conjunction that emphasizes their symbolic unity. This pairing may represent a merism. Thus, "thorns and thistles" might symbolize all forms of ungodliness, a suggestion that, while speculative, aligns with their consistent negative connotations in Scripture.

The New Testament builds on this imagery, portraying thorns not only as a symbol of ungodliness but also as a manifestation of its effects on human life—particularly through anxiety, temptation, and a lack of fruitfulness.

Christ's Use of Thorn Imagery

Jesus expands the symbolic meaning of thorns in *The Parable of the Sower*, where they represent spiritual hindrances. Thorns, in this context, choke out a plant's potential to produce fruit, illustrating the destructive power of worldly anxieties and the deceitfulness of wealth:

Matthew 13:22

22 What was sown among the ***thorns*** is
when someone hears the word, but the

---

[38] 2 Samuel 23:6

[39] Genesis 3:18; Exodus 22:5; Judges 8:7,16; 2 Samuel 23:6; Isaiah 32:13; 33:12; Jeremiah 4:3; 12:13; Ezekiel 28:24; Hosea 10:8; Psalm 118:12

[40] Genesis 3:18; Hosea 10:8

> anxieties of this age and the
> deceitfulness of wealth choke the word,
> and so it produces nothing.

This passage draws on the Greek word *akantha* (*ἄκανθα*, AH-kahn-thah), the Septuagint's consistent translation of the Hebrew *qotz*. This linguistic continuity bridges the Old and New Testaments, reinforcing the metaphor's theological significance. Just as the Hebrew Scriptures depict thorns as obstacles to spiritual flourishing, Jesus uses them to illustrate the internal and external challenges that hinder faith. In this light, thorns symbolize both ungodly people and the destructive thoughts and distractions that infest the soul.

The symbolic meaning of *qotz* in these passages sheds light on its first mention in *The Fall of Man*, where thorns and thistles emerge as part of the curse following humanity's fall. They symbolize the fractured relationship between humanity and creation and also foreshadow the broader biblical theme of opposition to God's purposes. This recurring imagery, with its associations of rebellion and resistance to God, finds its ultimate expression with the thorny crown placed on Christ's head during the Crucifixion.

The Crown of Thorns

The crown placed on Christ's head during the Crucifixion is rich with symbolism but can only be seen now that we understand the Scriptures' symbolic use of thorns. While the adversary in the wilderness sought to persuade Jesus to accept ungodliness within His soul by yielding to temptation, Christ's earthly adversaries could do no more than futilely place the symbols of ungodliness on the God of all creation. This act, intended as mockery, serves instead as a testament to Christ's unassailable holiness and His victory over the world. In the thorny crown, we see a profound transformation of this symbolism: the sinless one confronts and conquers the consequences of sin, not as a bearer of its curse but as the healer of human nature.

The ungodliness that is symbolized in the imagery of thorns and thistles results in a judgment—not from God but as a natural consequence of our choices.

The Judgment That Follows Thorns and Thistles

The book of Hebrews continues the imagery of thorns and thistles, using them to illustrate spiritual barrenness and judgment. In Hebrews 6:4–8, those who fall away after receiving God's grace are compared to land that produces thorns and thistles:

Hebrews 6:4, 6a, 8

4 Regarding those who were once enlightened, who tasted of the heavenly gift, became partakers of the Holy Spirit,

6 but then fell away, it is impossible to renew them again to repentance!

8 Yet if it bears ***thorns*** and ***thistles***, it is rejected, close to being cursed; and its end is to be burned.

Here, thorns and thistles echo the cursed ground of Genesis, symbolizing the spiritual unfruitfulness of those who reject God's grace. The apostle's use of this imagery underscores its allegorical connection to the Fall narrative, portraying the natural consequences of rebellion against God: a self-imposed separation from Him.

Thorns, Thistles, and Divine Judgment

Understanding the significance of these symbols requires a closer look at the ancient Near Eastern perspective on divine judgment. Biblical authors often describe events permitted by God as if He directly caused them. For example, Pharaoh's hardening of the heart and Micaiah's declaration, "The Lord hath put a lying spirit in the mouth of all these thy prophets,"[41] reflects the ancient understanding that if God allows something to occur, it is ultimately within His sovereign purpose.

This perspective does not absolve human responsibility but emphasizes that rebellion produces inevitable consequences. The Hebrew word *avon* (עון, ah-VOHN) embodies this dynamic, interweaving its threefold understood meanings: iniquity, guilt, and punishment. Unlike *hete* (חטא, KHEYT), meaning "sin," and *pesha'* (פשע, pe-SHAH), meaning transgression, *avon* represents a habitual state of sin that resists repentance and results in judgment.

Divine judgment, then, often manifests as the natural outgrowth of human choices. By separating ourselves from God's protection, we expose ourselves to the consequences of sin, effectively becoming the authors of our own punishment.

While many Christians have long regarded sin, transgression, and iniquity as synonymous, we can now recognize that they are not. With this understanding of their differences, we can further explore an example that illustrates just how distinct these three categories of wrongdoing are, as well as how we are the authors of our own judgment. This is evident in the generational impact of iniquity.

Generational Impact of Iniquity

The Scriptures describe iniquity as carrying a unique punishment that is never applied to sin and transgression. The consequences of iniquity affect descendants down to the third and fourth generations.[42] I have developed a theoretical explanation as to why iniquity, an ingrained habitual sin, is passed to the third and fourth generations, while sin and transgression are not. My

---

[41] 1 Kings 22:23

[42] Exodus 20:5; 34:7; Numbers 14:18; Deuteronomy 10:5

conjecture is that ingrained habitual sin affects our epigenetics, which may then be passed to subsequent generations.

Scientific evidence suggests that trauma, stress, and environmental factors can result in epigenetic changes that impact subsequent generations,[43] and by logical extension, habitual sin—through the trauma, stress, and dysfunction it causes—might fall within this scope of inheritable effects.

This understanding underscores that it is not God actively imposing the consequences of our iniquities upon our children and grandchildren; rather, it is the natural outgrowth of human choices and biological processes at play here. These patterns, whether inherited biologically or culturally, emphasize the urgent need for repentance to break cycles of sin that can evolve into iniquity before they harm both us and our descendants.

Ultimately, divine judgment reflects the natural consequences of life apart from God's will. Yet, God's sovereignty ensures that even the outcomes of rebellion serve His redemptive plan. While thorns and thistles symbolize rebellion and judgment, the imagery of trees offers a hopeful contrast. Unlike thistles, which are inherently barren, trees possess the potential to transform—moving from fruitlessness to fruitfulness. This dual potential mirrors humanity's spiritual journey, where repentance and grace lead to renewal, while neglect results in decay.

Trees: A Symbol of Transformative Nature

The transformative nature of trees can be seen in *The Parable of Balaam*, where he compares Jacob's tents to cedars and aloes.[44] These trees, known for their strength and fragrance, evoke a sense of blessing and divine favor. Yet, in the context of the idolatry that soon follows—when some Israelites fall into sin with the

---

[43] See endnote: Epigenetic Transmission of Stress and Trauma Across Generations.

[44] Numbers 24:5–6

daughters of Moab—this imagery reveals a sobering reality. Just as some trees fail to produce edible fruit, so too can people stray from God's path, becoming spiritually barren despite their earlier promise.

Similarly, in *The Parable of the Fig Tree*, Jesus portrays the ongoing potential for change:

Luke 13:8–9

8 The gardener answered, "Lord, let it be for this year also, until I dig around it and fertilize it.

9 If it bears fruit, fine; but if not, after that, you can cut it down."

This parable illustrates the themes of judgment and mercy. The barren tree risks being cut down, but the gardener steps in, providing one last chance for change. This careful tending embodies the belief that even a seemingly unproductive life can find renewal through repentance and divine grace.

These examples illustrate the tree's distinctive function as a representation of humanity's spiritual state. Whether fruitful or barren, the tree signifies the dual potential for growth or decline, mirroring each individual's ability to change. Similar to trees, we can flourish when we remain grounded in God's care or fade when we stray. Therefore, the tree metaphor reminds us of the care we must exercise in remaining reliant on Christ, the true Vine in whom we must always stay grafted and bear fruit.

Faith as Fruitful Land vs. Spiritual Barrenness

The imagery of fruitful land versus barren ground in Hebrews 6:6–8 captures the spiritual consequences of faithfulness versus rebellion. The author compares those who have "tasted the good word of God" to land that "absorbs the rain . . . and brings forth a crop," symbolizing a faith that bears fruit and grows through divine teaching.

In contrast, those who "fall away" are likened to land yielding only "thorns and thistles," symbols of spiritual barrenness and rebellion. This imagery ties directly to the Genesis curse, where thorns and thistles represent the consequences of humanity's fall into sin. The cursed land mirrors the condition of the soul that rejects God's grace, destined for judgment and destruction.

With a deeper understanding of the symbolism behind various types of plant life, the reader of this passage in Hebrews should now notice something subtle yet significant. The author remarks about those who fell away that "it is impossible to renew them again to repentance!" He is not saying they cannot repent but rather that they won't. Thus, they are compared to thorns and thistles, which lack the nature of a fruit tree that can alternate between being fruitful and barren. The author's choice of imagery is not without purposeful nuance.

The agricultural metaphor in the book of Hebrews also echoes *The Song of Moses*, where rain symbolizes the divine teaching that descended from above to fall upon the people below. Like rain falling on the land, God's word reveals the condition of the heart—whether it produces fruitful growth or is overrun by weeds, thorns, and thistles. Together, these passages emphasize the stark contrast between spiritual fruitfulness and barrenness, urging readers to remain faithful and cultivate a life of faith that yields a rich harvest.

To fully understand these metaphors, we need to consider their original cultural and historical context. For the ancient Jewish audience, the imagery of different types of plant life was not just poetic flourishes or decorative stage props. Rather, they carried layers of meaning rooted in their shared language and culture's symbolic framework.

Harmonizing Timeline Discrepancies

Understanding the symbolic meaning behind each plant type enables us to address the timeline discrepancies in the creation accounts. We uncover how these symbols resolve the apparent contradictions by examining the symbolic layers rather than relying solely on a literal interpretation.

Let's begin by examining Genesis 2:5, which at first glance may seem illogical. However, the verse contains deep symbolism, so let's reset the stage and review these key points with clarity:

Genesis 2:5

5 No ***shrub*** of the field was yet in the earth, and no ***herb*** of the field had yet sprung up, for the Lord God had not caused it to rain upon the earth, and there was no man to till the ground.

The Absence of Shrubs and Herbs: Its Symbolic Meaning

Why does the text emphasize the absence of shrubs and herbs before the rain? Given that rain wasn't physically necessary—since mist watered "the whole face of the ground" and a river flowed out of Eden to water the Garden—what is the significance of mentioning rain?

To understand this, we must revisit an earlier point: the formation of man and the breathing of life into him. This act symbolizes God's selection of Jacob out of all the peoples on the earth, granting him both His presence and His Law, which *The Song of Moses* described as rain falling upon the tender grasses below. While comparing the giving of the Law to breathing life into man may seem like a stretch, we should remember that our Lord, in John 6:63, states, "The words I speak to you are spirit, and they are life."

Therefore, this verse in Genesis 2:5 describes the condition of mankind prior to the giving of the Law. The statement about the absence of shrubs and herbs, or the suggestion that they were mere seedlings yet to sprout, can be understood symbolically. Shrubs, often thorn-bearing, represent unprofitable servants, while herbs symbolize profitable servants.

Distinctions in Spiritual Readiness Before the Law

Before the rain, there was no distinction between profitable and unprofitable servants. Without the Law, how could there be? There are no servants at all—profitable or unprofitable. It is only after the rain falls that we can see which seeds will grow into life-giving herbs and which will become thorn-bearing shrubs, hindering the growth of others.

A person's true nature remains concealed until they receive the Law and the Spirit of God. It is only by responding to the message that one's character becomes apparent—as either fruitful, like nourishing herbs, or unfruitful, likened to thorns and thistles.

Thus, the Law acts as rain, facilitating the growth of seeds and revealing their true essence. This insight clarifies why *The Creation of Man* narrative includes what previously seemed an insignificant detail about what had not yet emerged. It becomes clear that this is not an irrelevant precursor to man being created in God's image but rather a crucial setup for the unfolding story.

From Barrenness to Fruitfulness

The symbolism of plant life in Genesis reflects humanity's spiritual journey, encompassing themes of rebellion, obedience, fruitfulness, and barrenness. Across these narratives, grass, herbs, shrubs, thorns, and trees serve as metaphors for the varying conditions of the human soul and its relationship with God. These symbols point to deeper truths about spiritual readiness, human responsibility, and divine grace.

Through these allegories, Genesis reveals that humanity is both the cultivated field and the cultivator tasked with bringing forth fruit in alignment with God's will. The Law and the Spirit act as rain, nurturing seeds and exposing their true nature. Just as profitable herbs sustain life, faithful servants embody the fruits of the Spirit, while thorn-bearing shrubs obstruct and hinder growth. These contrasts underscore the importance of remaining steadfast in faith, rooted in Christ, the true Vine.

The variations in the creation timeline further illustrate the inadequacy of literal interpretations, inviting us to uncover the allegorical richness of the text. Rather than discrepancies, these differences reveal a unified message: the journey from chaos to order, rebellion to restoration, and barrenness to fruitfulness reflects God's transformative work in humanity.

By understanding these plant metaphors in their ancient context and tracing their symbolism across Scripture, we see how the Genesis narratives connect to the broader biblical message. From the curse of thorns in the Fall to the redemptive imagery of Christ's thorny crown, these symbols remind us of both the consequences of sin and the hope of renewal through repentance and grace.

As we reflect on these timeless truths, may we strive to be fruitful in our faith, aligning ourselves with God's purpose and cultivating lives that bear witness to His glory. This exploration of plant symbolism sets the stage for deeper engagement with the allegories of Genesis, allowing us to uncover their profound relevance to our spiritual lives today.

Chapter Ten

Separating the Dry Land

On the third day of creation, God separated the dry land from the waters, an act that also carries deep symbolic significance. This chapter explores the meaning behind these events, examining how they represent the establishment of sacred space and spiritual renewal. By analyzing key Hebrew terms and their usage throughout Scripture, we uncover rich symbolism that extends from ancient Israel to contemporary Christian practice.

The Symbolic Meaning of Dry Land

As with other parts of the Genesis narrative, this depiction of dry land need not be understood as a literal event but as a symbolic representation of God's establishment of order and sacred space:

Genesis 1:9–10

9 And God said: 'Let the waters under the heaven be gathered together unto one place, and let the ***dry land*** appear.' And it was so.

10 And God called the dry land Earth, and the gathering together of the waters called He Seas; and God saw that it was good.

We have already observed how the allegory's use of "division" signifies the separation of the sacred from the profane.

This concept appears again in the Creation narrative, where the dry land being separated from the waters symbolizes God setting apart a holy space for His chosen people.

Dry Land as Sacred Space

This idea is manifest in a key Hebrew word, *yabashah* (יבשה, yah-bah-SHAH), which is translated as "dry land." To fully appreciate its significance in the Creation story, we must explore how it is used elsewhere in Scripture.

It appears sixteen times in the Hebrew Bible. To gain a clearer understanding of its significance beyond the Creation narrative, we'll examine its usage in other contexts. Excluding the two instances that directly reference creation, we find *yabashah* used in the following ways:[45]

- six times in Exodus: twice when speaking of pouring the blood from the Nile onto dry land, four times when relating how the Israelites passed through the sea on dry land
- once in Joshua to recount how the children of Israel passed upon dry land from the plains of Moab, through the Jordan River, to the Promised Land[46]
- once in Isaiah, when God speaks of pouring out water upon a dry land
- once in Nehemiah to recall the Exodus
- twice in Jonah, as a place of safety from the sea
- once in Psalms, in recalling the Exodus event

---

[45] Exodus 4:9; 14:16, 22, 29; 15:19; Joshua 4:22; Isaiah 44:3; Jonah 1:13; 2:11; Psalm 66:6; Nehemiah 9:11

[46] Joshua 4:22

Through these examples, *yabashah* consistently emerges as a place of divine deliverance—a refuge from the surrounding chaos. This pattern prepares us to explore its deeper spiritual significance. Dry land can symbolically represent any safe, habitable place on earth. However, in the Hebrew Bible, its usage consistently appears in instances where God is delivering or guiding His chosen people or servants. It is a symbol of divine protection and separation from the forces of chaos that threaten life and order.

Water as a Symbol of Chaos

In allegorical terms, the "gathering of waters" represents more than physical oceans; it symbolizes the chaotic, idolatrous lands out of which Israel was carved. Just as waters embodied disorder in the ancient Near Eastern imagination, these nations—steeped in idolatry—threatened to overwhelm God's sacred order.

Many ancient Near Eastern cultures, including Mesopotamian, Canaanite, and Egyptian civilizations, portrayed chaotic waters as primordial forces that existed before creation, embodying disorder and danger. Given this shared understanding of water's symbolism, it would be shortsighted to believe that an allegory's reference to the seas must take on its literal definition.

From this pattern, the dry land in the Creation account represents more than just the earth emerging from the water. It symbolizes the physical preparation of a sacred space—the land of Israel—where Jacob could dwell as God's "Mine own treasure from among all peoples"[47] and a "kingdom of priests, and a holy nation."[48]

---

[47] Exodus 19:5; Deuteronomy 7:6; 14:2

[48] Exodus 19:6

Dry Land as a Spiritual Crossing

Beyond its literal meaning, *yabashah* carries a deeper, metaphorical significance: the transition from chaotic waters into a new life and relationship with God. This is clearly seen in the biblical accounts of the Israelites crossing both the Red Sea and the Jordan River on dry land. These crossings symbolize leaving behind a life of idolatry that seeks the things of this world and moving into a new relationship with both God and oneself.

This same symbolism is applied in the New Testament, where Paul likens the crossing of the Red Sea to baptism:

1 Corinthians 10:1–2

1 Now I do not want you to be ignorant, brethren, that our forefathers were all under the cloud: all passed through the sea;

2 and they were all baptized into Moses in the cloud and in the sea.

The Israelites' journey through the sea is a precursor to Christian baptism, where believers pass through the waters, leaving behind their old lives, and emerge onto dry ground, beginning a new life in Christ. The same imagery is present in the baptism of Jesus, who, after emerging from the waters and stepping on dry land, enters the wilderness—a parallel to Israel's journey through the wilderness after its "baptism" in the Red Sea.

However, in recapitulating the wilderness experience of the children of Israel, Jesus distinguishes Himself in the face of temptations by not bowing down to a false god. Again, His life is a retelling of the Exodus story but exemplifies what that story should have looked like.

This parallel between Israel's exodus and the Christian journey illuminates a profound truth: the concept of dry land as a place of spiritual transformation extends beyond ancient history into our present spiritual lives.

Metaphor for Spiritual Renewal

Thus, dry land in the Creation narrative also serves as a metaphor for spiritual renewal. Just as Israel's journey began with a crossing through the waters onto dry land, so too does the Christian journey begin with baptism, marking the start of a long path toward purification and illumination. We enter our wilderness of temptation not to engage in the temptations we encounter but to be purified of them.

Setting aside a sacred space without a people to live therein in obedience would be meaningless. For this reason, this Genesis passage uses a second rare term that suggests this requirement.

"Being Gathered" as a Symbol of Obedience

Having seen how *yabashah* represents the carving out of a sacred space for spiritual transformation, we turn to another distinct Hebrew word within the same verse, Genesis 1:9, cited above: *qavah* (קוה, kah-VAH). This is yet another *dis legomenon* within an inclusio, and it means "to be gathered." This Hebrew *niphal* (simple passive) verb appears only twice in the entire Hebrew Bible—once in Genesis 1:9 and again in the book of Jeremiah, where it is used to describe the gathering of nations unto Jerusalem:

Jeremiah 3:17

17 At that time, they shall call Jerusalem
The throne of the Lord; and all the
nations ***shall be gathered*** unto it, to the
name of the Lord, to Jerusalem; neither
shall they walk any more after the
stubbornness of their evil heart.

The use of *qavah* in Genesis suggests that this gathering symbolizes more than a physical act; it reflects the gathering of God's people into a sacred space where they receive His teachings and walk no "more after the stubbornness of their evil heart." This unique word choice, especially in light of Jeremiah 3:17, underscores the deeper spiritual meaning of the Creation allegory. It is not merely about forming physical order but about humanity's transformation: leaving behind the stubbornness of self-will to open their hearts to God's guidance.

Deeper Meaning of Deliberate Word Choices

There are many words that convey the idea of gathering—the primary ones being *qavatz* (קבץ, kah-VAHTS) and *asaf* (אסף, ah-SAHF), each appearing over one hundred times. Again, when there are more commonly used words that could have been employed, but the rarest word is chosen to be included in an allegory, one must ask himself, "What is the real meaning behind this word?"

While inclusios can be purely coincidental, in this case, however, the fact that Jeremiah conveys the same message of a gathering out unto a holy place should prompt the reader to consider the connection.

To answer the question, "What is this dry land?" we can now understand it as symbolizing the establishment of the land of Israel, a sacred space prepared for God's chosen people. This interpretation underscores the value of tracing rare and uncommon words through Scripture to uncover deeper meanings. By following this linguistic trail of *yabashah* and *qavah*, we can gain a clearer understanding of the spiritual significance behind the Creation narrative as it relates to "dry land" and "to be gathered."

A Symbol of Divine Order and Spiritual Renewal

The emergence of dry land from the waters in Genesis symbolizes more than physical creation. It represents the establishment of sacred space—a refuge from chaos where God's chosen people can dwell. This symbolism echoes through biblical history, from the Exodus to the crossing of the Jordan, each instance reinforcing the transition from turmoil to divine order.

This imagery transcends time, finding new expression in Christian baptism and believers' ongoing spiritual journeys. The dry land becomes a metaphor for spiritual renewal, marking new beginnings and closer communion with the divine.

Understanding this allegorical lens offers valuable insights into contemporary spiritual life. It reminds us of the importance of sacred spaces—both physical and metaphorical—where we encounter the divine. For Orthodox Christians, this includes the parish we attend as "dry land" in the midst of the surrounding confusion. Moreover, it encourages each of us individually to become a sacred space, free from the confusion that disturbs the world around us.

Therefore, the dry land of Genesis stands as a timeless symbol of God's ongoing work of creation and redemption in human hearts and communities, bridging ancient text with lived spiritual experience.

Chapter Eleven

Celestial Bodies and Divine Governance

On the fourth day of creation, there was another division of light and darkness, but it differed from that of the first day. While the light created on day one was not tied to any celestial body, the light on day four depended on the creation of the sun, moon, and stars to separate day from night:

Genesis 1:14–17

14 And God said: "Let there be lights in the firmament of the heaven to divide the day from the night; and let them be for signs, and for seasons, and for days and years;

15 and let them be for lights in the firmament of the heaven to give light upon the earth." And it was so.

16 And God made the two great lights: the greater light to rule the day, and the lesser light to rule the night; and the stars.

17 And God set them in the firmament of the heaven to give light upon the earth . . .

Before we delve into the significance of the fourth day, let's briefly recall the events leading up to it. On the first day, God created light and separated it from the darkness, a symbolic prelude to the divine separation of good from evil. On the second day, God established the waters above and below, preparing the heavens and earth to receive divine grace, much like how the Law would later "rain down" upon Israel. The third day marked the emergence of dry land, symbolizing the establishment of Israel as a nation to be known as the Promised Land.

Now, on the fourth day, the celestial bodies—sun, moon, and stars—represent not just the creation of physical lights but also the divine order and governance.

Harmonizing Light and Darkness Against Day and Night

A literal interpretation of Genesis raises apparent contradictions, such as the separation of light and darkness on day one, even though the celestial bodies essential for marking day and night are not created until day four. This prompts the question: How could light exist without the sun, and how could night occur without Earth's rotation away from a light source?

Instead of attempting to reconcile these challenges through scientific or mystical means, an allegorical reading offers a more consistent and meaningful interpretation. The light and darkness of day one symbolize a spiritual separation, representing order emerging from chaos and Israel's separation from the darkness of Egypt. In contrast, day four introduces the celestial bodies as symbols of rulership and divine rhythm within creation.

The Creation narrative is a perfect allegory of Israel's journey from chaos into divine order. After the separation of land from the seas on the third day, the establishment of rulers on the fourth day reflects God's intention to bring both physical and spiritual order to His people. The sun, moon, and stars are not merely markers of the seasons but powerful symbols of the divine governing order of Israel—and, ultimately, the world—under God's reign.

Joseph's Dream and Celestial Governance

The creation of the celestial bodies should remind us of Joseph's dream, which reflects this same theme of divine administration through its imagery:

Genesis 37:9–10

9 And he dreamed yet another dream, and
told it to his brethren, and said:
"Behold, I have dreamed yet a dream:
and, behold, the sun and the moon and
eleven stars bowed down to me."

10 And he told it to his father, and to his
brethren; and his father rebuked him,
and said unto him: "What is this dream
that thou hast dreamed? Shall I and thy
mother and thy brethren indeed come to
bow down to thee to the earth?"

In this dream, Joseph's family is depicted as celestial bodies, with his parents symbolizing the sun and moon and his eleven brothers representing the stars. This imagery foreshadows the leadership of the twelve tribes of Israel, destined to inherit the Promised Land. Similar to how the heavenly bodies in Joseph's dream reflect the roles within Jacob's family, the creation of the sun, moon, and stars on the fourth day indicates the divine order that would be established for God's people.

Celestial Symbols of Governance Across Cultures

The symbolic significance of the sun, moon, and stars was not unique to Israel. Ancient civilizations across the world, from the Egyptian to the Mayan and Aztec empires, revered celestial bodies as symbols of divine rulership. In Egypt, the sun was embodied in Ra, the moon in Thoth and Khonsu, and the Pharaohs believed they would ascend to become circumpolar stars, continuing to rule from the heavens after death. Many cultures shared this belief in celestial bodies governing the earth: the Greeks, Romans, Norse, Chinese, Persians, and others. These civilizations often believed that either their rulers became stars or that the stars sanctified their rulership.

Understanding these ancient beliefs provides context for interpreting the Bible. If we ignore this key fact, we risk reading the Bible's references to celestial bodies too literally. The ancient audience of Genesis would have understood the deeper symbolic meanings of these references and perceived them not as mere descriptions of physical phenomena but as representations of governance, order, and divine authority.

The Symbols of Divine Order throughout the Scriptures

Recognizing the symbolic meaning of heavenly bodies transforms our interpretation of many biblical passages. Earlier, I suggested that understanding the creation and Fall allegories would unlock the meaning of many passages throughout the Bible. Now, with this symbolic understanding of the fourth day of creation, we gain new insight into passages like those in Revelation:

Revelation 6:13–15

13 The stars of the sky fell to the earth, like a fig tree dropping its unripe figs when it is shaken by a great wind.

14 The sky was removed like a scroll when it is rolled up. Every mountain and island was removed from its place.

15 At this, the kings of the earth, the princes, the commanding officers, the rich, the strong, every slave, and every free person sought to hide themselves in the caves and the rocks of the mountains.

A literal interpretation of these verses might seem perplexing, particularly given that stars, being vastly larger than the Earth, could not physically fall to it without catastrophic consequences. However, an allegorical perspective reveals a more coherent meaning: these verses depict the fall of governmental powers. The synonymous parallelism between verses 13 and 15 underscores this symbolism. The stars falling from the sky represent the downfall of earthly rulers, offering a striking metaphor for political and spiritual upheaval.

Marking the Signs, Seasons, and Calendar

In Genesis 1:14, we read: "And let them be for signs, for seasons, and for days and years." This single statement has stirred much discussion, particularly as it is often interpreted without reference to the cultural and societal structure of Israel during the wilderness period and afterward. Understanding this structure deepens our connection to the Creation story as a reflection of Jacob's journey through the wilderness, as later alluded to in *The Song of Moses*. Here, it is the twelve tribes—designated as signs and seasons—who embody the order and meaning of the created world.

Reflecting on the twelve tribes as representations of the stars created on the fourth day, as seen in Joseph's dream, we can see how each tribe's placement around the Tabernacle was both intentional and symbolic. Positioned according to divine instruction, Judah, Issachar, and Zebulun encamped on the east; Reuben, Simeon, and Gad to the south; Ephraim, Manasseh, and Benjamin to the west; and Dan, Asher, and Naphtali to the north.[49]

While the Bible does not explicitly link each tribe to a specific month, later Talmudic and rabbinic traditions suggest an association between the tribes' arrangement and the sequence of months in the Jewish liturgical calendar. Judah, for example, is

---

[49] Number 2:3–31

connected to the month of Nisan, Issachar to Iyyar, Zebulun to Sivan, and so on. Thus, each tribe symbolically presides over its corresponding month and its feasts so that as the calendar unfolds, it reflects a progression through the twelve tribes, with each one governing and embodying the spiritual character of its month's observances.

The Hebrew Bible itself offers only anecdotal inferences regarding these tribe-month associations. For example, Judah is often given primacy among the tribes, particularly in leadership, associating it with the first liturgical month of Nisan—the month in which Passover, the Feast of Unleavened Bread, and Bikkurim (First Fruits) occur. Given that the Messiah comes from the tribe of Judah, His connection to these foundational feasts is significant.

Zebulun is associated with the month of Sivan, which falls under the feast of Shavuot (Feast of Weeks). This feast celebrates the giving of the Torah at Mount Sinai. In rabbinic and Talmudic tradition, Zebulun is metaphorically linked to this feast through its renowned partnership with Issachar, where Zebulun supported Issachar's Torah study by engaging in commerce and trade, sharing in the spiritual rewards.

Admittedly, this tie between the tribes and the marking of signs and seasons is the most tenuous, as we have no direct scriptural confirmation for it. Instead, it relies on inferences and later Talmudic and rabbinic writings. As such, I won't go through each of the twelve tribes trying to justify their tribe-month associations. Nevertheless, I include it, as many Eastern Orthodox Christians may be unfamiliar with these Jewish traditions, and they are worth considering for the broader symbolic context they provide.

Having provided this background, let's return to what is actually confirmed in the Scriptures.

The Twelve Stones: A Memorial of Divine Order

This theme of celestial symbols representing divine order is echoed after the Israelites crossed the Jordan River. As a reminder of the twelve tribes, the Israelites set up twelve stones as a memorial,[50] marking the divine structure of tribal rulership that had been established long before during the days of Jacob and his sons.

This act of remembrance foreshadows not only the governance of Israel but also the eternal rule of Christ and His twelve apostles. These patterns of divine order are repeated throughout Israel's history, emphasizing that the establishment of order was not a one-time event in Genesis but a recurring theme in God's relationship with His people.

Cycles of Divine Governance: Abraham, Exodus, and Jesus

To further illustrate the theme of divine governance, let's explore three major cycles in Israel's history that reflect the events of the Creation narrative: Abraham's journey, the Exodus, and Jesus's ministry.

Abraham's Journey:

Abraham began his journey from Ur to Canaan, making this the first historical event symbolically linked to the creation of dry land emerging from chaotic waters. His journey led him out of an idolatrous land, after which God separated for him a strip of land that would be known throughout time as the Promised Land, foreshadowing Israel's future inheritance.

Later, his grandson, Jacob, would give birth to twelve sons whose descendants would inherit and govern the land. Again, these are symbolized as the sun, moon, and stars in Joseph's dream.

---

[50] Joshua 4:20

The Exodus:

Moses led the Israelites out of Egypt and toward the Promised Land, reflecting the separation of dry land from the chaotic waters of an idolatrous nation. He initiated the establishment of order by assigning land to the twelve tribes, confirming Joseph's vision of his brothers as rulers alongside him.

Jesus's Ministry:

Jesus, the ultimate fulfillment of Israel's promise, reflects this cycle once more. His return from Egypt, and His later selection of twelve disciples, mirrors the governance of the twelve tribes and completes the cycle of divine order. It was completed because His kingdom is an eternal one that will never end.

The Pattern of Divine Order

From the opening verses of Genesis, the Creation story sets a pattern of divine order that unfolds throughout Scripture and the history of Israel. The sun, moon, and stars, created on the fourth day, are more than mere physical lights; they are symbols of God's authority and the structure He established to govern His people.

This symbolism extends from the twelve tribes encamped around the Tabernacle to the twelve stones set as memorials and ultimately to the twelve apostles who lay the foundation of a new spiritual kingdom.

Across generations, this theme of sovereign reign through a body of twelve reappears in Abraham's journeys, Israel's deliverance from Egypt, and Jesus's ministry, each echoing the original Creation account's movement from chaos to divine order. By tracing the connections between celestial symbols, Israel's tribal structure, and prophetic visions, we see that God's blueprint for governance is both purposeful and timeless.

These patterns remind us that the order established in creation continues to shape God's relationship with His people. As we encounter these symbols in Scripture, we are encouraged to understand them not only as historical or cultural references but as reflections of a divine reality that governs both the heavens and the earth. Ultimately, this divine order points to God's eternal presence, guiding His people toward unity, purpose, and the fulfillment of His eternal kingdom.

Chapter Twelve

Creation and Dominion Over All Creatures

Living Creatures: A Precursor to Man

By the fifth day of creation, all of the groundwork had been laid in preparation for the creation of a man in God's image. However, let's consider the earlier days of creation, where a special land was set aside for Israel, followed by the establishment of a governmental system. Given this sequence, it may not seem logical to see the introduction of creatures that swarm in the sky and the waters.

It took me a considerable amount of time to grasp its purpose here. I had to move beyond my strong reliance on analyzing distinct Hebrew words in hopes that their usage outside the allegorical context would clarify their meaning within the allegory. While this interpretive method revealed the passage's true meaning, I also had to rely on my Eastern Orthodox understanding of the hesychastic path of purification to see its true place within this narrative.

Swarms and "After Their Kind"

At first glance, the introduction of swarming creatures may seem unrelated to creating a man in God's image, but, as we will see, this progression mirrors the journey of the soul toward purity:

Genesis 1:20–22

20 And God said: "Let the waters swarm
with ***swarms*** of living creatures, and let

fowl fly above the earth in the open firmament of heaven."

21 And God created the great sea-monsters, and every living creature that creepeth, wherewith the waters swarmed, ***after its kind***, and every winged fowl ***after its kind***; and God saw that it was good.

22 And God blessed them, saying: "Be fruitful, and multiply, and fill the waters in the seas, and let fowl multiply in the earth."

This chapter will also cover the first half of day six, which refers to the creation of all land-dwelling animals:

Genesis 1:24–25

24 And God said: "Let the earth bring forth the living creature ***after its kind***, cattle, and creeping thing, and beast of the earth ***after its kind***." And it was so.

25 And God made the beast of the earth ***after its kind***, and the cattle ***after their kind***, and everything that creepeth upon the ground ***after its kind***; and God saw that it was good.

Once again, we find Hebrew words that are only used in specific contexts. They are *sheretz* (שרץ, SHEH-rehts), meaning "swarms," as seen in verse 20, and *leminah* (למינה, leh-mee-NAH), meaning "after its/their kind." As we have done in other instances, here we will also examine their usage outside the allegories to discover their meanings within the allegories themselves.

The Creation of Clean and Unclean Creatures

It is important to recall, based on our previous analysis of other Hebrew phrases such as "And there was evening, and there was morning" and "God divided," that each day of creation illustrates a distinct contrast between the clean and unclean, order and chaos, the holy and the profane.

We begin with the understanding that this symbolism will also manifest itself through the events of each day. This is helpful because, in any interpretive endeavor, narrowing the boundaries of possibilities reduces our chances of coming up with a completely off-target conclusion. The question then becomes, "What do the *swarms* and the other animals made *after its/their kind* represent in relation to the contrasting themes just mentioned?"

The word swarm, *sheretz*, appears fourteen times[51] outside the Creation allegory.

- once in the Flood story, where it is stated the swarming creatures would perish
- twelve times in Leviticus, declaring which creatures are either clean or unclean to touch or eat
- once in Deuteronomy to reiterate that winged swarming creatures are unclean

The phrase "after its/their kind," *leminah*, appears twenty-one times[52] outside the Creation allegory.

- seven times in the Flood story, speaking of the kinds of animals to be brought on board

---

[51] Genesis 7:21; Leviticus 5:2; 11:10,20–21, 23, 29, 31, 41–44; 22:5; Deuteronomy 14:19

[52] Genesis 6:20; 7:14; Leviticus 11:14–16, 19, 22, 29; Deuteronomy 14:13–15, 18; Ezekiel 47:10

- nine times in Leviticus, declaring which creatures are either clean or unclean to touch or eat
- four times in Deuteronomy to reiterate which animals are clean and unclean
- once in Ezekiel to refer to many kinds of fish

These occurrences highlight that the focus of the fifth day and the early part of the sixth day aligns with the distinction between clean and unclean animals. While *leminah* broadly categorizes living creatures, its frequent use in Leviticus and Deuteronomy associates it with ritual distinctions.

Although the Creation narrative does not explicitly mention "clean" and "unclean," the repeated use of these terms and their Levitical resonance suggests that the act of creating animal life was inherently one of separation and functional assignment.

By invoking language that anticipates Levitical categorizations, the author(s) of Genesis may have intentionally invited readers to connect the Creation account with the ritual laws of Leviticus, emphasizing a divine order that encompasses both creation and covenantal life.

Man's Dominion Over All Creatures

This naturally prompts the question, "How do these classifications of animals relate to the gradual, step-by-step process culminating in the creation of a man in God's likeness?" To answer this, we must consider the event that follows, as it ties back to this division of animals after their kind:

Genesis 1:26

26 And God said: "Let us make man in our
image, after our likeness; and let them
have dominion over the fish of the sea,
and over the fowl of the air, and over

> the cattle, and over all the earth, and
> over every creeping thing that creepeth
> upon the earth."

These verses must be understood as a cohesive unit to grasp their full message. In fact, it could be argued that this series of verses surrounding man's creation form a chiastic structure—a literary device often used in biblical texts where themes are presented in a mirror-like structure (A-B-C-B-A), designed to highlight the center as the main focus or central axis.

Understanding Chiastic Structures

Chiasm plays a crucial role in understanding biblical texts. These literary devices are invaluable for interpreting passages that might otherwise elude comprehension. Recognizing chiastic structures can be challenging, as often only one half of the structure is immediately apparent, while the other remains unclear.

The power of chiastic structures lies in their mirroring effect. When we identify and understand one half of the structure, it can illuminate the meaning of the more symbolic or complex half. This mirroring can take various forms, including synonymous, antithetical, complementary, thematic, and many more.

While some authors have identified certain chiastic structures related to the creation of animal life leading up to the creation of man, they have often missed its deeper purpose by focusing solely on the narrative as a literal account of the creation of physical life forms. To uncover its full significance, we must move beyond the surface of the translation, beyond reading it as mere history, and beyond limiting our analysis to the Hebrew words and their allegorical meanings.

Here, the creation of "man in our image" serves as the central axis (B), framed by the creation of clean and unclean animals and God's directive for humanity to exercise dominion over them.

A (v. 24-25): Land animals "after their kind" are created

B (v. 26a): God makes man in His image

A' (v. 26b): Man is given dominion over all creatures

This thematic chiastic structure makes it very clear the author(s) intended to emphasize an inseparable connection between being created in God's image and the discernment of clean and unclean (indicated by the use of "after their kind," reminiscent of Levitical categorizations) leading to dominion over these divisions.

However, how does gaining mastery over physical creation alone achieve this? The answer is that it doesn't! This passage must be understood in a more spiritual light, pointing to humanity's inner transformation and the path toward reflecting God's likeness.

Gaining Dominion through Purification

We must recognize that being made in God's image is deeply connected to the path of purification—a process that cleanses unclean thoughts and desires that obstruct the inner stillness that Christians seek. In this light, we turn to the Eastern Orthodox understanding of the hesychastic path to fully appreciate the spiritual depth of this passage. Without this shared mindset passed down to us through tradition, it is virtually impossible to come away with the right interpretation of the text, highlighting how Sola Scriptura falls short once again.

Through this journey, we become masters of our inner kingdom rather than being overrun by wild, unclean beasts. It is our responsibility to transform the inner wilderness—full of dangerous, venomous creatures—into a Garden of Eden, free from thorns, thistles, and unclean animals. This is the land we are called upon to till and over whose beasts we are to gain dominion.

Naming as an Act of Dominion

Not only does the first allegory, *The Creation of Sky and Land*, address this need for man to exercise dominion, but it is repeated in *The Creation of Man*:

Genesis 2:20

20 And the man gave names to all cattle, and to the fowl of the air, and to every beast of the field; but for Adam there was not found a help meet for him.

In ancient Semitic cultures, it was common for men to be given new names by their new sovereign. This practice is frequently seen in the Scriptures. For example, God gave Abram and Sarai new names, changing them to Abraham and Sarah. King Nebuchadnezzar also gave new names to Daniel and his companions. Joseph's name was changed to Zaphenath-paneah by the Pharaoh, and Pharaoh Necho renamed Eliakim to Jehoiakim. This practice continued into the times of Christ, when He gave Simon a new name, Peter. Our Lord also gave to James and John the name Boanerges, meaning "sons of thunder."

By renaming an individual, the conquering king symbolically asserted control over that person's identity and future. The new name may even describe the person's new role and relationship with his king.

The Symbolism of Dominion Over Animals

Similarly, the act of naming the animals represents a symbolic exercise of dominion. This naming is not merely about assigning literal names to every species. Instead, it signifies the recognition and mastery of one's inner chaos—the animal-like passions that dwell within the human soul. To truly become a man in God's image, one must first confront these inner demons of thought and passion, name them, and thereby begin the process of gaining dominion over them.

If we look at these verses holistically, they present a deeper connection: God separates the clean and unclean animals and then immediately says, "Let us make man in our image." Within the same sentence, being made in God's image is directly tied to the command, "Let them have dominion over . . . ," which is followed by a list of the categories of creatures.

A purely historical reading of this account raises the question, "Why is God's first act after creating man to grant dominion over all animal life?" This sequence of events seems disjointed and lacks deeper spiritual significance, especially in light of the impracticality of a literal understanding.

The Impracticalities of Naming All Animals

A symbolic interpretation of Man naming the animals becomes far more plausible when we consider the impracticalities of a literal reading. (Here, I refer to the first human as "Man" because, at this point in the narrative, he is called "the man"; most translations have not yet identified him as "Adam.")

Today, we know of approximately 11,000 bird species and 6,400 mammal species. Even if Man spent only one minute naming each, it would take nearly 290 hours. If we account for additional time to create sketches or notes to accompany the names—without which the list would be useful only to Man—the process could stretch into months. This also assumes that the "Adamic" language had developed sufficiently to facilitate written communication.

While some might argue that Man didn't need to document the names, this raises additional questions: How could Man recall thousands of names, many of which might never be used again? What was the point of naming animals if those names weren't recorded for future generations?

Additionally, from a historical perspective, the Adamic language quickly faded from history, given that, using the Bible's genealogy as literal, less than two thousand years had passed between Man's creation and the Tower of Babel. Consequently, any names assigned would lose relevance within several generations. God, anticipating the Tower of Babel and the resultant language division, would have realized that literally naming animals in a language destined to be lost would have little significance.

If naming all creatures were a literal and vital task, we would expect some preservation of those names, yet no such record exists. This strongly suggests that the true meaning lies elsewhere.

Rather than a logistical task, Man's naming of the animals is best understood as a metaphor for humanity's spiritual journey. Just as a sovereign renames a subject to signify control over their identity and future, Man's act of naming the clean and unclean animals symbolizes self-mastery—the process of recognizing and gaining dominion over one's inner passions and thereby taming the inner landscape. In so doing, he becomes a man made in God's likeness.

Dominion Restored: The Path to Reflecting God's Image

The creation of animals and their categorization "after its/their kind" on days five and six, culminating in the creation of humanity, reflects an allegory that was clearly intended to be a lesson in spiritual transformation. Through linguistic analysis and theological reflection, we see that this narrative is not merely about biological life forms but about the journey of the soul toward inner purification.

The division of clean and unclean creatures parallels the separation of base desires from higher aspirations, a process essential for humanity to fully conform to God's image. The act of naming animals symbolizes mastery over one's inner passions, echoing the patristic teaching that taming beastly impulses leads to the restoration of the divine image within us. In this light, the dominion described in Genesis 1 is not a practical command to rule over physical creatures but a spiritual call to transform the wilderness of the soul into a garden of divine reflection. This interpretation, grounded in tradition and supported by the hesychastic path, offers a timeless reminder of God's desire that we become a man in His image, reflecting His holiness through a life of purity and self-mastery.

Part Five

The Fall's Actors

Before looking at the actors in these allegories, it's important to review what we've discussed thus far. Having laid out most of the pieces of this puzzle in logical groupings, we can now do what was impossible before: explain all the symbolism in a day-by-day structure, describing it and what it means in relation to the life of Israel. This will be the first focus of this series of chapters.

While we have uncovered a lot of the allegorical meaning behind Adam and Eve, there is still more to examine regarding how I reached the conclusions presented and who these characters symbolize in the historical context of Israel. Therefore, we will delve into Adam, Eve, and the serpent in some depth.

Chapter Thirteen

Reviewing the Journey

Resetting the Picture

The message of the creation allegories is rooted in *The Song of Moses*, which describes how God encountered Jacob, representing the nation of Israel, in the wilderness. The text refers to finding Jacob in "a desert land, and in the waste, a howling wilderness," using the Hebrew word *tohu*. This word, meaning "chaos" or "formlessness," is a *dis legomenon*, appearing only twice in the entire Torah. Additionally, *tohu* serves as an inclusio, bookending the Law by connecting Genesis 1:2, where it describes the chaotic state of the earth before creation, to Deuteronomy 32:10 in *The Song of Moses*. This intentional framing underscores the thematic link between creation and the wilderness journey.

We also saw how the connection between these bookends of the Law is further strengthened by a second inclusio, *rakhaf*, which means "to hover over." Together, these two terms—*tohu* and *rakhaf*—frame the narrative, emphasizing a transition from chaos to divine intervention.

Before the acts of creation begin, Genesis 1:2 describes the earth as "unformed," "void," "darkness," "the deep," and "the waters"—all of which are understood to be synonymous symbols of a state of chaos. The introduction of the Spirit of God hovering over this chaos portends that something is about to change drastically, which indeed happens on day one of creation.

On day one, the narrative doesn't disappoint as it next tells us God said, "Let there be light." This is the moment in the history of mankind when God appeared to Moses in the burning bush on Mount Sinai. There, God gave Moses the command to lead His people out of Egypt: ". . . that thou mayest bring forth My people, the children of Israel, out of Egypt." This exodus was the allegorical act of separating light from darkness: the nation of Israel, God's chosen people, from the dark, idolatrous land of Egypt.

This parallel sheds light on the apparent delay in the Creation narrative between the emergence of light and its separation from darkness. It mirrors Israel's gradual establishment as a light to the world, set apart from the spiritual darkness of Egypt. Just as night transitions slowly into day, the journey of the children of Israel from darkness to light was a process, not an instant transformation. The Scriptures underscore this allegorical division, presenting Israel as the light that reveals God's truth to all nations:

Isaiah 42:6

6 I the Lord have called thee in righteousness, and have taken hold of thy hand, and kept thee, and set thee for a covenant of the people, for a light of the nations . . .

On day two, the next step was to create a firmament, or dome, that would divide the waters above from the waters below. According to ancient Near Eastern cosmology, the waters above the dome are considered holy since they are in God's presence. It is from these waters above that the rains fall, which the Scriptures always refer to as the bestowal of God's grace and the nurturing of life.

In *The Song of Moses*, we are told, "My doctrine shall drop as the rain." It is therefore not unreasonable to infer that the "waters above" were symbolic of the giving of the Law from atop Mount Sinai, where only the most holy among men were allowed to ascend.

On day three, we see upon whom the sacred rain was destined to fall—the dry land gathered from the surrounding chaotic waters. As explored in the chapter "Separating the Dry Land," the Hebrew word for "dry land," *yabashah*, conveys a specific meaning of safe passage amidst the surrounding chaos.

This act of separation symbolizes God establishing the land of Israel, a sanctuary for His people to worship Him free from the confusion and idolatry of the surrounding nations. Here, God provided a home for a holy and fruitful people, symbolized in the allegory by "grass, herb yielding seed, and fruit trees." This metaphor is echoed in Isaiah 5:7, where the children of Israel are described as "the plant of His delight." The inclusion of plant life following the gathering of the dry land emphasizes that Israel is both its land and its people.

The events of day three follow a natural progression. Building on day two, where the "waters above" symbolized the heights of Mount Sinai, we see that from this elevated point, the Law—like rain—descends upon the plant life below. As previously discussed, the descriptions of plant life on day three serve as metaphors for humanity. Here, they signify the children of Israel as the first recipients of this life-giving rain, which would eventually flow outward, nurturing all mankind.

On day four, God created the sun, moon, and stars, symbolizing the establishment of an orderly structure for both the holy land and the people gathered within it. These celestial bodies, often understood as symbols of governing powers, represent the leadership needed to maintain divine order within the community. It is fitting that before the Israelites entered the land, Moses began assigning the territorial inheritance to the twelve tribes named after Jacob's sons.

Further insight into the symbolism of celestial bodies comes from Joseph's dream, in which Jacob's sons are represented as stars and his parents as the sun and moon. This helps clarify the distinction between the separation of light and darkness on the first day and the creation of celestial bodies on the fourth.

On the first day, light symbolizes divine order triumphing over chaos, while the fourth day introduces the instruments to sustain that order. The sun, moon, and stars are described as "ruling over the day and night, dividing light from darkness."

Similarly, Israel's leaders, like these celestial bodies, are tasked with discerning between righteousness and disobedience, guiding the people in obedience to God's Law. Their role mirrors that of the heavenly bodies: to govern wisely, separating the light of divine truth from the darkness of sin.

For many, the apparent discrepancy between the creation of light on the first day and the establishment of day and night on the fourth day has caused confusion. This allegorical perspective clarifies the meaning: God establishes divine order first and then provides both celestial and communal structures to sustain and uphold that order.

On day five, God created the creatures of the air and sea, describing them with the term *leminah*, meaning "after its/their kind." In Genesis, this phrase highlights the diversity and categorization of living beings within an ordered creation. However, *leminah* later appears in Leviticus and Deuteronomy, where it is used to distinguish between clean and unclean animals. This repeated use suggests that the author(s) of the Creation allegory may have intended readers to draw a connection between these passages.

As previously discussed, the Law's separation of clean and unclean creatures serves a deeper purpose. It teaches worshipers to make similar distinctions within themselves, separating what is clean from unclean in their thoughts, desires, and passions. This internal discernment mirrors the external order of creation, inviting humanity to align their inner lives with God's divine order.

On day six, with the order of creation firmly established—light overcoming darkness, waters divided, land emerging to sustain life, and celestial bodies governing time and seasons—God turned to the pinnacle of His creative work: "a man in our image." The narrative shifts from preparing an environment to placing its steward within it. Man is made in God's image, entrusted with dominion over all living creatures. Yet, this dominion is not merely physical; it carries the transformative responsibility to discern and gain dominion over the clean and unclean, both in creation and within Man's own heart.

The Pinnacle of Creation

After examining the six days of creation, we now focus on the key figures of Adam, Eve, and the serpent. This leads us to a critical question: If the aspects of creation—light, darkness, land, water, plants, celestial bodies, and the waters above and below—act as symbols hinting at deeper spiritual meanings, should we interpret Adam, Eve, and the serpent literally within this complex framework of allegory?

By viewing these figures through the same symbolic lens, we unlock deeper insights into the divine narrative of transformation and spiritual growth. Just as the Creation allegory reveals God's vision for humanity, these characters illuminate meaningful truths about our relationship with God and the inner journey toward reflecting His image.

Summarizing the Purpose of Creation

The creation allegories ultimately reveal God's vision for humanity: a people who could rise above base instincts and chaotic thoughts to become something greater. For this transformation to occur, God illuminated their minds, breathed life into them, and shaped them in His image. However, this growth required a controlled environment—one safeguarded from external influences that could pull them back into enslavement to their beastly passions, a recurring struggle throughout Israel's history.

To address this need, God established a land set apart, as isolated as possible from the surrounding idolatrous nations—a place where His people could grow, learn, and thrive under His guidance. That land was Israel, a name given to Jacob, the son of Isaac and grandson of Abraham.

The journey from chaos to order would take time and a commitment from God to dwell among His people. His presence, along with the Law, would teach them how to divide light from darkness and order from chaos. Rituals would help internalize these teachings, transforming their behavior and creating lasting change. Their very nature would be altered as they learned to embrace what is good and reject what is evil, allowing them to reflect God's image.

This transformative journey begins with Adam, the allegorical figure representing the first image of God. He is the starting point on humanity's path to being shaped and transformed into God's likeness, reflecting His divine nature and purpose.

Chapter Fourteen

Adam: The Scriptures' Silence

An Unexpected Absence

Before we examine the linguistic evidence surrounding Adam's name or rethink the biblical evidence for his identity, we must confront a question that is seldom asked but impossible to ignore once it is raised: Why is Adam absent from the rest of the Hebrew Bible?

If Adam were understood by the ancient Israelites as the literal first human being—the father of all humanity, the one whose single act of disobedience brought death and separation from God into the world—we would expect him to appear throughout the Scriptures as a towering figure of theological significance. We would expect the prophets to invoke his name when calling Israel to repentance. We would expect the psalmists to reflect on his fall when meditating on human frailty. We would expect the wisdom writers to draw lessons from his story when counseling the righteous.

Yet none of this occurs. The silence is comprehensive, spanning centuries of prophetic writing, poetry, wisdom literature, and historical narrative. And it demands an explanation.

Surveying the Canon

Let us walk through the major divisions of the Hebrew Bible and observe what we find—or rather, what we do not find.

In the Torah itself, after the creation and Fall narratives conclude, Adam never reappears as a figure of moral or theological significance. The remaining books of the Law—Exodus, Leviticus, Numbers, and Deuteronomy—are concerned with Moses, the covenant, the giving of the Law, and the journey through the wilderness. Not once does the text look back to Adam as a cautionary example or a theological reference point. Moses is the central figure, and the people's relationship with God is framed entirely through the covenant at Sinai, not through any primordial event in Eden.

In the Former Prophets—Joshua, Judges, Samuel, and Kings—the pattern continues. These books recount the history of Israel from the conquest of the land through the monarchy and into exile. They invoke Moses repeatedly. They reference Abraham, Isaac, and Jacob as the patriarchs of the covenant. They hold up David as the standard against which all subsequent kings are measured. But Adam is never mentioned, not even in passing.

The Latter Prophets present the most striking absence. Isaiah, Jeremiah, Ezekiel, and the Twelve Minor Prophets are deeply concerned with sin, repentance, exile, and restoration—the very themes that later theology would trace back to Adam's fall. Yet not one of these prophets invokes Adam's name when diagnosing Israel's condition or calling them back to faithfulness. Isaiah speaks of humanity's rebellion but never traces it to a single ancestor. Jeremiah laments the broken covenant but frames it entirely in terms of Israel's relationship with the Law given at Sinai. Ezekiel, remarkably, uses Eden imagery extensively but treats it as a metaphor for beauty and divine favor—never as the historical setting of a literal first man whose disobedience explains the human condition.

Even Isaiah, when he promises restoration, compares the renewed land to Eden but does so without any reference to Adam as a historical figure. The garden functions as a symbol, not a biography.

Some readers may object that these prophetic references to Eden presuppose the existence of the Genesis narratives in their current form, and therefore argue against a post-exilic dating for those narratives. However, this conflates a cultural tradition with a specific literary composition. As we explored earlier in this book, the Hebrew word *'eden* (עדן) is etymologically linked to the Sumerian word *edin*, meaning "plain" or "steppe." The concept of a primordial garden of divine abundance was part of the cultural vocabulary of the ancient Near East long before any biblical author set it down in the form we now possess. This tradition was known since the days of Abraham, whose own origins lay in Mesopotamia, where such imagery was deeply rooted. Ezekiel's and Isaiah's references to Eden draw upon this ancient, shared heritage—they do not require the carefully crafted Genesis narrative, with its dual inclusios, its precise use of *badal* and *tohu*, and its allegorical actors representing Moses and the congregation, to have already existed. The raw material is ancient. The specific composition we find in Genesis 2–3 is another matter entirely.

The Writings—Psalms, Proverbs, Job, Ecclesiastes, Song of Solomon—offer perhaps the most telling silence of all. The psalmists meditate extensively on human mortality and frailty: "As for man, his days are as grass; as a flower of the field, so he flourisheth." Yet they never attribute this condition to Adam's transgression. The author of Ecclesiastes reflects at length on death, futility, and the human condition without once looking back to Eden as the explanatory framework. Job, in the most profound exploration of suffering in the Hebrew Bible, never invokes Adam's fall to explain why humanity suffers. These writers had every reason to reference Adam if they understood him as a historical figure—and they did not.

Compare this silence to the treatment of Moses, whose name appears approximately 770 times across the Hebrew Scriptures, or David, who is referenced over a thousand times, or Abraham, who appears roughly 175 times. These are figures the biblical authors treated as historically real and theologically indispensable. They returned to them constantly because they understood them as actual persons whose lives carried enduring lessons for God's people.

Adam receives no such treatment. His absence is not a minor gap; it is a pattern of omission so thorough that it constitutes evidence in its own right.

Over 500 Witnesses

Before proceeding further, it is worth pausing to consider a statistical reality that frames everything we have observed. The Hebrew word *adam* (אדם) appears over five hundred times in the Hebrew Bible. In the overwhelming majority of these instances, it is translated simply as "man" or "mankind." It functions as a common noun, no different from how we might say "man is mortal" or "the nature of man."

The handful of cases where translators render it as a proper name—"Adam"—are interpretive choices, not linguistic necessities. Even the one verse sometimes cited as a prophetic reference to Adam—Hosea 6:7—is rendered by the JPS, KJV, and other respected translations as "like men," confirming that the choice to read a proper name here is a matter of translator preference, not linguistic necessity. There is no definite article shift, no patronymic, no "son of" construction—none of the markers that Hebrew typically uses to signal a personal name. The translators simply decided, based on context and tradition, that certain occurrences referred to a specific individual. Centuries of reading followed that decision without questioning it.

This means the prophets and wisdom writers were not ignoring a historical figure. They were using the word *adam* constantly—always meaning humanity in general. The very concept of a singular individual named Adam may be a later imposition on a text that never intended one. We will examine the full linguistic evidence in the next chapter.

When Adam Became a Person

If Adam is absent from the canonical Hebrew Scriptures as a developed historical figure, when does he first appear as one? The answer is revealing: in the pseudepigraphal literature of the Second Temple period.

Texts such as the *Life of Adam and Eve* (also known in its Greek version as the *Apocalypse of Moses*) and the *Book of Jubilees* are the first works to give Adam a fully realized biography—a personality, a narrative arc, dialogues, and a detailed account of his life after the expulsion from Eden. In 2 Esdras, Adam is explicitly named as the one through whom sin entered the world, and his transgression is treated as a historical event with cosmic consequences. The Wisdom of Solomon alludes to death entering the world through envy, though even here Adam is not named directly.

These texts were composed during or after the Second Temple period—well after the Babylonian exile. They represent a theological development, not an original tradition. The authors of these works took the allegorical figure of the Genesis narratives and historicized him, transforming a Hebrew common noun embedded in a spiritual allegory into a character with a life story.

This historicization then passed into early Christian theology, where Paul's typological use of Adam in Romans 5 and 1 Corinthians 15 was read through the lens of this already-developed tradition. By the time the Church Fathers wrote their commentaries, the historical Adam was so deeply embedded in the theological imagination that questioning his existence seemed unthinkable. But the canonical Hebrew Scriptures—the very texts that contain the creation and Fall narratives—do not share this assumption.

There is an observable timeline: the Genesis narratives present *adam* as a common noun within an allegory. The pre-exilic prophets and wisdom writers use the word hundreds of times as "man" without ever treating it as a personal name. The pseudepigraphal authors, writing centuries later, convert this common noun into a biographical character. And subsequent Christian theology inherits and builds upon that conversion. Recognizing this trajectory does not diminish the spiritual truths contained in the Genesis narratives; rather, it invites us to recover the depth of meaning that the allegorical reading was always designed to convey.

Why the Silence Matters

The implications of this survey are significant. If Adam were the historical first human being, the father of all humanity, we would expect him to be referenced throughout the Hebrew Scriptures with a frequency and reverence proportional to his theological importance. Instead, we find a silence so complete that it can only be explained in one of two ways: either the entire prophetic and wisdom tradition of Israel inexplicably ignored its most foundational figure, or the Genesis narratives were never understood by their authors or original audience as the biography of a literal individual.

The first explanation strains credulity. The second invites us to recover the allegorical depth that the narratives were designed to convey—a depth that, as we have seen throughout this book, reveals far more about God's relationship with His people than any literal reading could offer.

This silence also raises a question we will explore later in the book: If the Genesis narratives reached their final form during or after the Babylonian exile, as many scholars believe, they were composed by a community that had just lived through the very pattern the allegories describe—fall, exile from God's presence, and the hope of return. The absence of Adam from pre-exilic literature would then have the simplest of explanations: the narrative, in the form we possess it, had not yet been written.

For now, what the silence tells us is this: the Hebrew Bible's own witness does not support the later tradition of Adam as a historical individual. What it does support, through the linguistic evidence we are about to examine, is a reading of *adam* as "man"—a collective figure representing humanity's relationship with God, its capacity for communion with Him, and its recurring tendency to choose its own counsel over His.

With this understanding in place, we are now prepared to examine the linguistic evidence surrounding Adam's name itself—evidence that confirms and deepens what the Scriptures' silence has already suggested.

Chapter Fifteen

Adam: The Challenges of His Name

Setting the Allegorical Framework

At the heart of this discussion is the understanding of Adam as an allegorical figure rather than a historical one. He represents Jacob, who in turn symbolizes the nation of Israel during a critical period in its history: the wandering in the wilderness after the Exodus. Within this framework, Adam and Eve are seen as symbolic representations of Moses and the children of Israel, respectively.

Before delving into Adam's allegorical significance, it is necessary to address the rejection of him as a purely historical figure, beginning with the implications of his name. Deconstructing the traditional view of Adam as a singular male figure is crucial—not only for unlocking the meaning of the allegories but also for reevaluating many inferred doctrinal beliefs that have emerged from these long-held misconceptions.

Adam: An Anachronistic Name

To fully understand the name "Adam," we must first set aside the assumption that "Adam" and "Eve" were the literal names of humanity's first ancestors. Viewing them as historical figures who lived more than 2,500 years before Moses raises a significant issue: These names could not have existed in their era. As Dr. John H. Walton explains in *The Lost World of Adam and Eve* (2015):

> Although I believe that Adam and Eve are historical personages—real people in a real past—these cannot be their

historical names. The names are Hebrew, and there is no Hebrew at the point in time when Adam and Eve lived.

The name "Adam" is, therefore, an anachronism, reflecting the language of the text's author(s) rather than any original name. In a pre-Hebrew or "Adamic" language, the figure's name likely carried a meaning similar to "Man," which later informed the Hebrew word *adam*.

For modern readers, it can be difficult to grasp how much language can change during the span of time that transpired from Adam to Moses. However, this phenomenon is not unique to Hebrew. English provides striking examples of how words can shift significantly in meaning and form over time.

Consider the word "knight," which began in Old English (450–1150 CE) as *cniht*, meaning "boy" or "servant." By the Middle English period (1150–1500 CE), the term had evolved to signify a "military servant" or mounted warrior. In modern times, the term "knight" has evolved to symbolize exceptional achievement and honor across diverse fields.

The title "Sir," bestowed through a knighting ceremony, is now granted to individuals from various backgrounds who have made outstanding contributions to their professions or society. Remarkably, this transformation has occurred in under two millennia, demonstrating how profoundly language can evolve.

When we adopt a literalist perspective and accept the biblical genealogies as accurate, it is reasonable to conclude that Adam would have lived in a period when such a word either did not exist in its recognizable Hebrew form or carried entirely different connotations. This raises further questions about how its translation was handled over time.

Transliteration vs. Translation

Translators of the Hebrew Bible faced a choice: preserve the sound of the Hebrew word through transliteration or convey its meaning in translation. By choosing transliteration, they cemented the view of *adam* as a singular proper name rather than as it was originally intended in its broader collective context. For the ancient Israelites, this would have been unthinkable. They instinctively understood *adam* to mean "Man" or "mankind," depending on context.

The Impact of Transliteration on "Adam"

This distinction is especially important in the creation and Fall narratives, where the Hebrew word *adam* functions as a collective identity rather than a specific individual. Treating it as a proper name in Genesis diverges from its consistent use elsewhere in Scripture, where it refers to humanity or groups of people with shared traits, such as the nation of Israel. Recognizing this bias opens us up to a fresh reading of the Genesis account, one that aligns with its allegorical depth and symbolic roles.

The Septuagint's Role in the Name Shift

In Western cultures, names are often adopted without consideration for their meanings. This practice, however, was foreign to the ancient Israelites. The shift toward names devoid of their original meaning began with the translation of the Hebrew Bible into the Greek Septuagint. The translators of the Septuagint transliterated names, preserving their phonetic sounds but discarding their meanings. As a result, subsequent generations inherited names stripped of the rich nuances they once carried for the original Hebrew audience.

Names as Mere Labels

This loss of meaning profoundly impacts modern readers. To illustrate, consider the difference between names with clear meanings and those requiring interpretation. If a parent names their child "Hope" or "Brook," the meaning is immediately evident. However, names like "Ron" (as in my case) require research to uncover their origins. For instance, "Ron" could derive from the Hebrew *ron* (רוֹן, ROHN), meaning "song" or "joy," or the Old Norse *Rögnvaldr*, meaning "ruler's counselor." Similarly, understanding biblical names often requires exploring their original Hebrew context.

The Challenge Left to Us

Unfortunately, transliteration has left us with the same investigative task for every biblical name. Most readers today do not research their deeper meanings, missing their cultural and theological significance. This issue is compounded by the fact that nearly all Bible translations render the text in the target language—except for names. For example, consider this verse in Genesis:

Genesis 21:5

5 And Abraham was a hundred years old,
when his son Isaac was born unto him.

Modern readers have little sense of what "Abraham" or "Isaac" meant to the Israelites. In their original context, these names would have been pronounced "ahv-rah-HAHM" and "yeets-KHAHK" and understood as "father of many" and "he will laugh." A translated version of this verse might read:

Genesis 21:5

5 And "father of many" was a hundred
years old, when his son "he will laugh"
was born unto him.

Transliteration Was Justified

This approach preserves names' symbolic and theological importance. However, the translators faced challenges that influenced their choice to transliterate. A single Hebrew name often requires multiple words to convey its meaning in another language, making translation cumbersome. Ancient Greek lacked punctuation marks, such as the quotation marks that I used to clarify "father of many" as a name. Consequently, transliteration became the practical choice, even at the cost of the name's original meaning.

The Inevitable Consequences

Transliteration has significantly influenced our understanding of Scripture, often obscuring the meanings that the names therein carried for ancient audiences, leading readers toward misguided assumptions and conclusions. Restoring these meanings enhances our grasp of the text's cultural and theological depth, revealing the deliberate design within the narrative. Names like "Abraham" were far more than labels—they were declarations of God's promises and purposes.

The Consistent Use of Adam in Scripture

The Hebrew word *adam* appears 526 times outside the Genesis allegories. In every instance, it is used in one of two ways:

1. To refer to all of humanity.
2. To represent a group of individuals with shared traits.

This consistency is significant. A core interpretive principle is to examine how a word is used throughout Scripture. If a term is consistently understood in a particular way but is translated uniquely in a specific text, it raises the possibility of translator bias.

The Creation of Man allegory diverges from the consistent use of *adam*, presenting it as a proper name for a single individual. This anomaly should prompt readers to question the tradition of translation. While newer translations often have access to better scholarship, many adhere to precedent to avoid criticism or rejection, perpetuating inherited biases.

Translators, similar to interpreters, are not immune to doctrinal biases; these factors can subtly affect the rendering of key terms. It is essential to approach translations with scrutiny, considering multiple perspectives to uncover the text's fuller meaning.

Why Adam Is Often Interpreted as Historical

What has led to the frequent portrayal of Adam as a singular historical individual? Two key factors rooted in the issue of transliteration versus translation have significantly shaped this perspective:

1. Biblical genealogies frequently use the transliterated form "Adam" instead of translating it as "Man." This choice has led readers to interpret the term as a proper name, reinforcing the notion of a single, unique individual.
2. St. Paul, writing in Greek and drawing from the Septuagint, also uses the transliterated form. His theological reflections, such as those in Romans and 1 Corinthians, have further solidified the understanding of "Man" as a historical figure in the Christian tradition.

These conventions have deeply influenced how Adam is understood in Genesis, embedding the idea of a singular historical figure into both interpretive and translation practices. This traditional interpretation often discourages readers from exploring the term's broader symbolic and collective significance, narrowing the richness of the Genesis narratives.

By recovering the Hebrew word *adam* as "Man," we open the door to a deeper understanding of the allegorical intent behind these foundational stories. For example, interpreting him as a collective representation of humanity rather than a singular individual shifts the focus from a single origin story to a broader exploration of humanity's role and relationship with God. This perspective invites us to engage with Scripture in a way that reveals its theological depth and enduring relevance.

Name Shift Alert

For this reason, I will focus on translating the Hebrew words *adam* and *khava* as "Man" and "Life" instead of the traditional "Adam" and "Eve." I acknowledge that this transition may initially unsettle some readers, but it is essential. It allows us to understand how ancient audiences might have interacted with these names, unbiased by the limitations of later transliterations.

Examining Man across Scripture

The literary limitations of the past no longer constrain modern readers, and I encourage Christians to explore all biblical names through their translated meanings to uncover greater nuance. Furthermore, making this shift will remind us of the significant influence translators have had on our perceptions and interpretations of biblical stories.

This shift also underscores a broader reality: the entire Bible comes to us through translation, a process inherently interpretive in nature. As Fr. George Mastrantonis explains in his article *The Bible:*

Its Original Languages and English Translations on the Greek Orthodox Archdiocese website (goarch.org):

> Translations of the Bible are very necessary, but are not sufficient for formulating dogmas and doctrines of the Church, which requires reference to the original languages. The translations depend upon the genius and knowledge of the translator in the selection of the proper words and phrases to render meaning as close as possible to the text of the original language. It is well-known that a new translation is more or less a new interpretation.

The phrase "as close as possible" perfectly captures the challenge of translating Scripture. A translation can never fully convey the richness and depth of the original text, and this limitation affects not only theologians but any reader seeking a deeper understanding of the Bible.

To better understand this challenge, let's consider how translation affects even the works of a well-known figure like Shakespeare. Imagine seventy translators—the same number traditionally associated with the Greek Septuagint—independently translating Shakespeare into Japanese. If their translations aligned perfectly, it might be celebrated as "the definitive Japanese version of Shakespeare." Yet even this would fail to capture the full genius of his works. Everyone would recognize the value of reading Shakespeare in English, as his wit, humor, and intricate wordplay come alive in ways that no translation, no matter how skillful, could fully capture.

Similarly, we would hesitate to trust a teacher who had studied Shakespeare only in Japanese, knowing their understanding would inevitably lack the depth and nuance provided by the original language. I use this non-theological analogy because deeply held religious beliefs can often blind us to the logic of explanations that challenge our established views, making it difficult to approach such ideas with an open mind.

Beyond linguistic precision, understanding the Bible requires immersion in the culture, structure, and geography of the ancient Near East. Just as understanding Shakespeare requires familiarity with the customs and contexts of his story settings, unlocking the depth of Scripture depends on viewing it through the lens of its original world. Without this cultural and historical lens, we risk imposing modern assumptions on ancient texts, distorting their meaning through the filters of translation and contemporary worldviews.

Engaging with the Bible in its original languages and cultural context allows us to gain a fuller understanding of its key figures and themes. Names, often reduced to mere labels in translation, come alive with symbolic significance, revealing layers of meaning that illuminate God's purposes. Through this deeper engagement, we rediscover the intentional richness woven into Scripture, allowing its message to illuminate our faith and understanding in a transformative manner.

Rethinking Our Assumptions

To challenge this prevailing view, we must critically examine the assumptions underlying it. Are the genealogies and St. Paul's references intended to be understood as historical accounts, or do they serve a theological or allegorical purpose? Addressing these questions requires a logical and methodical reevaluation of traditional interpretations. By doing so, we open the door to fully appreciating the rich allegorical depth embedded within the Genesis narratives.

Chapter Sixteen

Adam: Rethinking Biblical Evidence

The belief that Man was a literal historical figure, largely based on his inclusion in genealogies where he is listed as "Adam," is frequently cited as evidence. However, this inference is misguided and overlooks the theological intent behind genealogies, which often have symbolic connotations and should not be regarded as historically accurate.

The Purpose of Genealogies

We will explore two pedigrees. The first is designed to show that omissions are purposeful because genealogies are primarily used in the Bible to convey spiritual truths. The second illustrates how, even in modern times, placeholder names are inserted when the real name(s) of ancestors are unknown.

Understanding the symbolic intent of genealogies helps us reframe Man's inclusion not as a record of a literal individual but as a representation of broader theological truths. Matthew's genealogy of Jesus provides a striking example of how biblical genealogies prioritize symbolism over completeness.

Exploring Matthew's Genealogy of Jesus

In Matthew chapter 1, we can see how accuracy is sacrificed in the recitation of a genealogy to convey spiritual truths. This genealogy, which extends from Abraham to Jesus, omits Ahaziah, Joash, and Amaziah, while Jehoiakim is not explicitly mentioned.

This omission is most likely intentional, aligning the genealogy with a symbolic structure of three sets of fourteen generations: from Abraham to David, from David to the exile in Babylon, and from the exile to Christ.

The Spiritual Structure of Matthew's Genealogy

Although this structure implicitly suggests the number forty-two by citing three groups of fourteen generations, the reader is left to do the actual math: 3 x 14 = 42. However, since David is included in two sets, the actual count is forty-one. The reader is left to infer that Jesus, found in the third set, is the fulfillment of the promised eternal King David. This reminds us that symbolism, not strict accuracy, takes precedence in biblical genealogies.

Fourteen: A Symbol of King David

Matthew emphasizes the numbers fourteen and forty-two, both carrying important symbolic weight. The number fourteen corresponds to David's name (דוד, dah-VEED); its Hebrew letters—daleth (4), vav (6), daleth (4)—combine to total fourteen. By structuring Jesus's genealogy into three sets of fourteen generations, Matthew underscores Jesus as the ultimate realization of the Davidic line, the eternal King foretold in the scriptures. We can sense the eternal nature of what is being presented through another number, three, which in the Jewish tradition signifies divine completeness, unity, and fulfillment.

Forty-two: A Symbol of Suffering and Redemption

The number forty-two also carries significant weight, symbolizing a time of suffering and fulfillment. As outlined in Numbers 33, the Israelites journeyed through forty-two encampments in the wilderness before Joshua brought them into the Promised Land. Similarly, Matthew outlines forty-two generations from Abraham to Christ, who guides His people into the everlasting Promised Land, the kingdom of heaven.

By examining other biblical texts, we find further evidence that the number forty-two symbolizes a period of suffering. For instance, Elijah's famine is described in Luke 4:25 and James 5:17 as lasting forty-two months, though the Old Testament states only that the famine ended in the third year.[53] This discrepancy suggests that Luke and James prioritized the symbolic significance of forty-two over strict historical accuracy.

This approach reflects a broader pattern among biblical authors, who often emphasized conveying spiritual truths over adhering to precise factual details. Similarly, in Revelation 11:2 and 13:5, St. John uses the same forty-two-month period to depict the great tribulation. These connections suggest that Matthew employs this symbolic number to portray Jesus as the one who brings ultimate redemption after humanity's prolonged journey of suffering and exile.

Biblical genealogies like this one convey deeper theological messages, often at the expense of historical precision. This is not an error but a deliberate choice, as their primary purpose is to communicate divine truths. This symbolic approach to genealogies is not unique to Scripture; similar methods are used in other disciplines, such as linguistics, where theoretical constructs serve to convey broader relationships.

The Genealogy of Semitic Languages

Allow me to illustrate another example with a "pedigree chart" from my studies of Semitic languages. Since we don't know the first Semitic language, it is simply the convention to use "Proto-Semitic" as a stand-in designator.

[53] 1 Kings 18:1

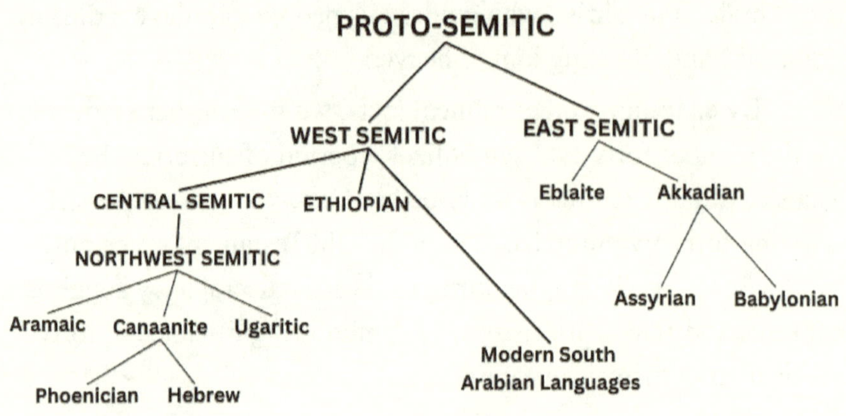

By examining the similarities and differences across various Semitic languages, linguists identified their relationships and inferred the probable existence of a Proto-Semitic language as their shared ancestor. While we don't know its actual name, the term "Proto-Semitic" serves as a theoretical construct to represent this ancestral language.

In this way, scholars construct "genealogies" of languages, adding theoretical placeholders and omitting unknown elements to create charts that convey broader relationships. Similarly, the appearance of "Adam" in a biblical genealogy does not necessarily mean he was a singular historical person. Genealogies in Scripture, like linguistic charts, are often shaped to convey theological or symbolic truths rather than strict historical accuracy.

Consequently, the inclusion of *adam*—better understood as "Man"—in a biblical genealogy should not be viewed as definitive proof of a literal individual. Much like the theoretical placeholders often used in genealogies, his presence may symbolically represent a "first man" whose specific identity remains unknown within humanity's lineage.

As we shall see next, these placeholder names may also effectively teach spiritual lessons, particularly when viewed in relation to Jacob's story.

Reconsidering Traditional Interpretations

From our previous discussion, we are then challenged to read any genealogy in which the name "Adam" is found and ask ourselves this question: Is this an actual historical pedigree, or is it symbolic? If we conclude it's symbolic, what could it mean? Let's consider where we first see such a genealogy.

Genesis 5:3

3 And Adam lived a hundred and thirty years, and begot a son in his own likeness, after his image; and called his name Seth.

It is worth noting that Life viewed Seth as a replacement for her lost son, Abel.[54] Seth was born when Man was 130 years old. Interestingly, Jacob was also 130 years old[55] when he reunited with Joseph, the son he thought he had lost decades earlier.

Could the parallel between Man receiving a new son at age 130 and Jacob reuniting with Joseph at the same age be a mere coincidence? This seems highly improbable, especially considering that Man lost Abel to the violence of his brother Cain, just as Jacob lost Joseph to the violence of his brothers. This connection suggests that the history of Man and Life mirrors Israel's history, with this particular detail in Man's genealogy pointing to a significant event in Jacob's story.

Both Man and Jacob experienced the restoration of a lost son: Man through Seth after Abel's death and Jacob through Joseph after decades of separation. The shared age of 130 likely holds symbolic significance as a Jewish number representing restoration and renewal.

---

[54] Genesis 4:25

[55] Genesis 47:9

This parallel reinforces the understanding that genealogies in Scripture serve a purpose far greater than recording historical details—they convey profound theological truths about restoration, loss, and God's redemptive plan for humanity.

Having explored how biblical genealogies prioritize theological symbolism over historical accuracy, we turn to St. Paul's writings. His epistles provide another key example of Man's role as a collective archetype. In examining Romans 5, we see how Paul intertwines historical, theological, and symbolic dimensions to present Man—representing Moses and the children of Israel—as the starting point of humanity's fall and Christ as the means of its restoration.

St. Paul's Understanding of Man

This section involves a deep theological exploration of St. Paul's understanding of Man. The non-scholar may prefer to skip the detailed discussion, as it is quite complex, and simply proceed to this chapter's last section, which summarizes how St. Paul viewed Man as a collective identity. This will not affect your understanding of the overall message.

Man and Christ in Paul's Theology

In the previous chapter, I noted a perspective that might lead readers to mistakenly perceive Man as a singular historical figure, influenced by his portrayal in the New Testament.[56] St. Paul's epistle to the Romans presents the most compelling opportunity to examine this claim in greater depth. Specifically, Romans 5 invites us to ask whether Paul understood Man as a literal historical figure or as an allegorical archetype representing humanity within the framework of ancient Jewish Scripture.

---

[56] Luke 3:38; Romans 5:14; 1 Corinthians 15:22,45; 1 Timothy 2:13–14; Jude 14

This exploration is essential for uncovering the deeper theological significance of Man's role in Paul's writings. While the discussion that follows is rich with theological insights, engaging with this complexity is necessary to fully grasp Paul's message.

Fortunately, the passage we will examine features a chiastic structure that significantly aids in unraveling this complexity. The reader may recall that we explored the structure and purpose of chiasm in the chapter "Creation and Dominion Over All Creatures," in case a review of these concepts is necessary.

Romans 5: The Contrast Between Man and Christ

Romans 5:12–21 contrasts the reign of disobedience and death brought into the world through "one man" against the obedience and life brought through "the one, Jesus Christ." We will begin, however, by examining the fourteenth verse, as it serves as part of the central axis of the passage:

Romans 5:14

> 14 Nevertheless death reigned from Adam until Moses, even over those who had not sinned in the likeness of the offense of Adam, who is a type of Him who was to come. (NASB95)

Paul uses the Hebrew-to-Greek transliteration *Ἀδάμ* (ah-THAM) to identify the first man, emphasizing the typological connection between Adam and Christ. This choice, however, may lead readers to view "Adam" primarily as an individual, potentially obscuring the broader archetypal significance in Hebrew thought.

When interpreting New Testament texts, it's crucial to consider the multifaceted nature of "Adam" in Paul's usage. This requires examining the Hebrew context and broader theological framework. Paul's presentation often blends historical and symbolic dimensions, portraying Adam as both a specific figure and a representative of humanity's shared identity.

We must consider then that this verse could easily be more properly rendered as follows:

Romans 5:14

14 Nevertheless death reigned from (the first) man until Moses, even over those who had not sinned in the likeness of the offense of (the first) man, who is a type of Him who was to come.

By inserting "the first," which admittedly places my translation more along the lines of what scholars refer to as "dynamic translation,"[57] we highlight that Adam allegorically represents the first man in Paul's typological argument. This interpretation aligns with Paul's depiction of him as the starting point of humanity's fall and Christ as the beginning of its restoration.

The connection is further reinforced in 1 Corinthians 15:45, where Paul refers to Christ as the "last Adam." My translation retains and emphasizes the implied antithetical parallelism[58] that I believe Paul intended. In presenting Adam and Christ as polar opposites, Paul emphasizes the contrast between death through Adam and life through Christ. Translating *Ἀδάμ* (ah-THAM) as "the first man" aligns with Paul's broader theological framework.

---

[57] Dynamic translation is a method of rendering biblical texts that prioritizes conveying the meaning of the original language rather than a word-for-word equivalence

[58] Antithetical parallelism, a poetic device commonly found in biblical literature, contrasts two opposing ideas within parallel lines, as in Proverbs 10:1: "A wise son brings joy to his father, but a foolish son brings grief to his mother."

A Chiastic Structure in Romans 5:12–17

To justify this understanding, we must consider this verse in the broader context of the passage (Romans 5:12–21), where we find this chiastic structure embedded:

- A (v. 12): Sin and death enter the world through Man.
  - B (v. 13): Death reigns, even without the law.
    - C (v. 14): Contrasts Man's disobedience against Christ's obedience.
  - B' (v. 15): Grace and life through Christ contrasted with Man's trespass.
- A' (v. 16–17): Justification and life enter the world through Christ.

This chiastic structure is notable for its central axis (C), which highlights the contrast between Man's disobedience and Christ's obedience. Understanding this structure reveals how the second half of the passage elaborates on the first, deepening its theological message.

The chiastic structure reflects Hebraic literary styles, even in Greek texts. Though the New Testament was written in Greek, its authors thought and articulated ideas through a Hebrew lens influenced by Aramaic public discourse and a liturgical life where the Scriptures were read in Hebrew. This was further enriched by daily experiences deeply rooted in Jewish traditions. Understanding these patterns reveals a deeper significance in the text, illustrating how Paul's theology bridges Jewish and Christian viewpoints.

The Cooperative Nature of Salvation

This contrast between Adam and Christ is not merely about two individuals; it reveals a broader theological argument about humanity's collective transformation in Christ. The Church Fathers affirm that this transformation is achieved through a cooperative process. As Fr. Dumitru Stăniloae explains in *The Experience of God, Volume 4, The Church: Communion in the Holy Spirit* (2012):

> This unity with and in Christ is not based only on the affirmation of a common faith that may have a subjective character; instead, it is experienced in the identical power that comes to the believers and the Church from Christ, who is found in the Church. Believers experience the faith with the same power, which is given to them for a life of purity.

In Eastern Orthodox theology, righteousness is not merely a legal declaration but an ongoing process of transformation through participation in Christ's life. This synergy between divine grace and human cooperation underscores the interconnected realities of sin, grace, and salvation.

Man and Collective Disobedience

If righteousness is achieved through the cooperative obedience of the Body of Christ, then disobedience—attributed to "one man" in the first half of the chiastic structure—must similarly reflect humanity's shared identity and culpability. This collective understanding mirrors the relationship between Moses and the congregation of Israel in their mutual failure to uphold God's Law.

Paul reinforces this concept of collective disobedience in Romans 5:12, stating, ". . . death spread to all because all sinned." Here, "one man" symbolizes not a solitary figure but the shared condition of humanity, emphasizing the universality of sin and its consequences.

The figures of Man and Life—Adam and Eve—foreshadow the experiences of both disobedience and redemption. In 1 Corinthians 15:45, Christ is described as the "last Adam," while Deuteronomy 18:15 foretells a prophet like Moses. Together, these scriptures establish an inferred triangulating link between Adam,

Moses, and Christ. Consequently, Adam serves as the symbolic counterpart to the historical figure Moses. Christ, in this context, emerges as the antitype of both Adam and Moses.

Summarizing Our Understanding of "Man"

Paul's writings reveal Man as an allegorical figure, representing Jacob and, by extension, the collective identity of Moses and the children of Israel. Similarly, Christ, united with the Church, embodies the new Man and Life—fulfilling the symbolic roles of Adam and Eve. Through this cooperative obedience, humanity finds life and righteousness restored.

Within this sacramental and communal framework, Paul's message shifts from the actions of a single individual to the collective fall and redemption of humanity. Man and Christ, as symbolic representatives, embody two communities: one fallen through disobedience, the other restored through grace. This echoes *The Song of Moses*, where Jacob represents the nation of Israel as a whole.

Ultimately, Adam's presence in genealogies and Paul's writings should not be understood as evidence of historicity. Instead, Adam serves as a symbolic figure, encompassing both humanity's fallen and redeemed states. By interpreting Man this way, we uncover a richer theological narrative—one that connects humanity's collective journey to God's redemptive plan.

Chapter Seventeen

Eve as a Collective Identity

In this exploration of biblical allegory, we delve into the multilayered symbolism of Man and Life, traditionally known as Adam and Eve. By examining their roles through an allegorical lens, we uncover deeper meanings that illuminate the relationship between God, His chosen mediators, and His people.

This interpretation reveals how these figures represent not just individuals but collective identities and spiritual truths that span from Moses and the congregation of Israel to Christ and the Church. As we journey through linguistic insights, scriptural connections, and theological reflections, we'll discover how this ancient narrative continues to offer relevant insights into obedience, transformation, and our collective journey toward unity with God.

Having established that "Man" represents Moses, the mediator of God's Law, we now turn to Life, whose identity is inherently tied to her counterpart. Life cannot be understood apart from Man; her role and purpose are realized within their union.

Allegorically, Man prefigures both Moses and Christ—figures who stand as singular leaders with distinct, standalone roles. However, Life symbolizes the collective existence that depends on their leadership. Just as the congregation of Israel relied on Moses to preserve its identity as God's chosen people, so too does the Church depend on Christ for its very being. Without Moses, the people of Israel might have assimilated into Egyptian culture and lost their divine purpose. Without Christ, there would be no Church, as its life flows entirely from Him.

Thus, Life must be seen as inseparable from Man, representing a complementary and collective identity. She is part of Man's body, symbolizing the unity and interdependence necessary for the life and purpose of God's people.

Life's Real Name

The name "Eve" is derived from the Hebrew *khava* (חוה, khah-VAH), which means "Life" and identifies her as "the mother of all living."[59] Over time, her name was adapted to fit the phonetics of different languages: transliterated into Greek as "Εὕα," into Latin as "Eva," and finally into English as "Eve."

By using the translated names "Man" and "Life," we uncover deeper symbolic meanings. Man symbolizes the mediator of God's Law and covenant, with Moses and Christ serving as his antitypes. Life, on the other hand, represents the people transformed by this Law—the vitality of the body, the Church, and the ancient congregation of Israel.

Beyond these two significant foreshadowings, Man also represents each of us in the need for every individual to cleave to obedience, just as Adam was commanded to cleave to Eve, which meant to help her abide in a state of obedience that would ensure eternal life in God's presence. This is the power of symbolism, wherein a single figure can represent many layers.

This interdependence is crucial: Without Life, the divine Law lacks recipients to embody its transformative power. Man, as a mediator, provides the Law, but it's through Life that this Law is lived out and transmitted. While Moses and Christ serve as individual antitypes of Man, they also represent a broader collective identity. This collective aspect only emerges through the presence of Life—the people who receive and manifest the Law.

---

[59] Genesis 3:20

Thus, Man and Life together symbolize the complete covenant relationship: the giver and the receivers, the leader and the led, united in fulfilling God's purpose. This interpretation reveals the profound interdependence between God's chosen mediators and His people in the unfolding of divine will throughout Scripture. In this relationship, individual figures often represent collective realities, as we will now explore.

Life's Synecdochical Meaning

In Scripture, a single figure often represents both male and female aspects, with the female typically symbolizing the collective life of a multitude. Paul employs this imagery in 1 Corinthians 12:27, describing the Church as the Body of Christ, with Christ as its head. He develops this theme further in his letter to the Ephesians:

Ephesians 5:31–32

31 This is why a man will leave his father and mother and will be joined to his wife, and the two will become one flesh.

32 This is a great mystery: I speak concerning Christ and the Church.

Here, Paul quotes Genesis 2:24, comparing the union of a man and his wife to the spiritual relationship between Christ and the Church—elsewhere compared to the Bridegroom and Bride. He identifies this as a "great mystery"—a profound truth revealed through divine inspiration.

Building on this typology, the symbolism becomes even clearer. In the context of the cited verse, "a man" represents divine leadership, embodied in Moses and ultimately in Christ. At the same time, "his wife" symbolizes the community united under that leadership—whether in the congregation of Israel or the Church.

This collective identity is also vividly illustrated in *The Creation of Man*, where Life is formed from Man's rib.

Examining the Symbolism of the "Rib"

The traditional understanding of Life's creation centers on the idea that she was formed from Man's rib. However, we will take a closer look at the original Hebrew to gain a more complex understanding of its true translation and symbolic meaning:

Genesis 2:22

22 And the ***rib***, which the Lord God had taken from the man, made He a woman, and brought her unto the man.

Here, "rib" is a translation of the Hebrew word *tsela* (צלע, tsey-LAH), which most often is properly translated as "side." Outside *The Creation of Man* allegory, this term is primarily used in biblical descriptions of the Tabernacle, suggesting a structural metaphor for humanity as a dwelling place for God. It appears thirty-eight times[60] outside this Creation allegory.

- nineteen times in Exodus—all in reference to the Tabernacle sides
- once in 2 Samuel in referring to a hillside
- seven times in 1 Kings in describing the walls and door panels of Solomon's temple

---

[60] Exodus 25:12, 14; 26:20, 26–27, 35; 27:7; 30:4; 36:25, 31–32; 37:3, 5, 27; 38:7; 2 Samuel 16:13; 1 Kings 6:5, 8, 15, 16, 34; 7:3; Ezekiel 41:5–9, 11, 26

- eleven times in Ezekiel in describing the side chambers of the temple

Given its consistent use in describing sacred spaces, many scholars see Man's rib, *tsela*, as having symbolic connections to the Tabernacle and Temple, underscoring its importance in the allegory. Moreover, it indicates Genesis 2:22 would be more accurately rendered as this: "And the ***side***, which the Lord God had taken from the man, made He a woman." This view goes back to at least the Talmudic period, when Rabbi Samuel bar Naḥman, in *Bereshit Rabbah 8*, expressed this same opinion.

This consistent use of *tsela* in sacred contexts implies that Life's creation from Man's side signifies more than biological origins; it points to humanity's role as a dwelling place for God, a theme carried forward in the Tabernacle and Temple.

The Tabernacle as a Metaphor for Man

The Tabernacle serves as a foreshadowing on multiple levels. It foreshadows Mary the Theotokos carrying the living Christ within her. St. Germanus of Constantinople, in his *Homily on the Presentation of the Virgin in the Temple*, makes this comparison:

> Today she who alone is called the new, god-like, purifying and mercy seat, not made by hands, (cf. Hebrews 9.11) for mortals who have drowned in floods of sin is presented to the mercy seat of the temple.

The *Orthodox Study Bible* (Nelson, 2008) expands on this to show how each of us must strive to be a tabernacle for God's indwelling:

> In time, the moveable Tabernacle of the wilderness is superseded by the permanent temple in Jerusalem. The temple, in turn, is superseded by Christ (Jn 2:18–21) and the Church, which is His Body (Eph 1:22, 23). Moreover, in Baptism, every

Christian becomes a Tabernacle, a dwelling place of the Holy Spirit.

Together, these reflections highlight that every Christian must aspire to become a living Tabernacle, pure enough for God to dwell within. The Tabernacle symbolizes perfected humanity, with its "two sides" representing the collective identity of Man, encompassing both male and female aspects.

On an individual level, the unity of Man and Life emphasizes that obedience is vital for attaining eternal "life" in God's presence. The term "Man" functions as a multilayered symbol, representing Moses or Christ as singular leaders or collectively symbolizing Moses and the congregation of Israel or Christ and the Church.

Interpreting this nuanced term requires careful discernment, as its meaning shifts based on context—whether it signifies an individual figure, a collective identity, or the unity between the two. This complexity showcases the depth of Scripture's allegory, inviting readers to engage more deeply with its meaning. Through this layered symbolism, an allegory can simultaneously convey multiple narratives using the same imagery.

A Symbol of Obedience and Disobedience

In this symbolic framework, Life represents the people of Israel. Just as they were called to obey the Law delivered through Moses, Life was expected to follow the divine command given through Man. The allegory of disobedience in Eden mirrors the children of Israel's failure to uphold their covenant, illustrating the consequences of spiritual rebellion, which brings separation from God and spiritual death.

When the people of Israel strayed from God through idolatry—much like Life's choice to eat the forbidden fruit—they experienced exile from His presence. This parallel highlights the universal challenge of obedience. Even today, we echo Life's doubt, questioning, "Did God really say . . . ?" When we elevate our personal interpretations above received tradition, we risk repeating her error: redefining right and wrong on our own terms rather than allowing God's Law to transform us.

This pattern persists both corporately and individually. In the Church, such attitudes result in disunity and fragmentation; as individual Christians, it fractures our souls, plunging us into further spiritual chaos. We might demand acceptance as we are, disregarding the transformative path God has given us. Yet transformation—becoming like Christ—requires humility and obedience.

Jesus addressed this very issue in His day, speaking to those who assumed their righteousness was complete:

Luke 5:31–32

31 Jesus answered them, "Those who are
healthy have no need for a physician,
but those who are sick do!

32 I have not come to call the righteous,
but sinners to repentance."

If we are unwilling to be transformed into Christ's image, assuming we are already perfect, the Church cannot fulfill its purpose in our lives. Just as Life's existence and purpose depended on her unity with Man, so too does the Church's life and purpose depend on its obedience and connection to Christ. Transformation requires both contrition and a commitment to following the path God has set—a path that promises true renewal.

Christ taught His followers that they must "lose their lives" to find true life. But what does it mean to "lose one's life"? It means surrendering the rebellion of our own opinions, ideas, and desires—a death of self-will. This was the very surrender that Life refused when she sought to determine good and evil for herself, shifting from obedience and life to disobedience and spiritual death, respectively. God did not forcibly cast her out of the Garden, the place of His presence; rather, she chose separation through her actions.

The urgency of obedience becomes clearer when we consider two instances of the command "to cleave," which we will now explore.

Cleaving Unto One Another: A Mutual Duty

The allegory of Man and Life emphasizes unity and reveals important insights about obedience and devotion. The biblical command "to cleave" vividly portrays this dynamic. Examining this command in Deuteronomy and Genesis provides a metaphor that reinforces the necessity of wholehearted commitment.

In Deuteronomy 30, God calls upon His people to choose life and demonstrates how cleaving to Him is inseparable from this choice:

Deuteronomy 30:19–20a

19 I call heaven and earth to witness against you this day, that I have set before you life and death, the blessing and the curse; therefore choose life, that you may live, you and your offspring;

20a to love the Lord your God, to listen to His voice, and ***to cleave*** to Him; for that is your life.

The Hebrew word *davaq* (דבק, dah-VAHK), meaning "to cleave," conveys more than mere attachment; it signifies an enduring, wholehearted commitment to God's will, implying consistent obedience. We also find this same Hebrew word in *The Creation of Man*:

Genesis 2:24

24 Therefore a man shall leave his father and mother and ***shall cleave*** unto his wife . . .

Here again, the use of *davaq* (to cleave) conveys a full act of devotion. Notably, Scripture emphasizes Man cleaving to Life, which can also be understood as Man cleaving to obedience, since obedience and life are inseparable. This highlights his responsibility as a leader to uphold and guide her spiritual well-being, encouraging a life rooted in obedience. This dynamic prefigures Moses' steadfast leadership of the nation of Israel during their rebellion in the wilderness and Christ's upholding of the Church through grace and truth.

The symbolism of Life being formed from Man's side, juxtaposed with Man's duty to cleave to his wife, reminds us of a fundamental truth: Man, as a foreshadowing of Christ, initiates His relationship with us, taking the first step before we are even aware of His presence. Just as Man's commitment established the foundation of their union, God's love precedes and sustains our connection to Him, inviting our response through obedience and devotion.

In the same way that Man gave of himself to bring Life to his body, Christ offered His body in sacrifice and raised it from the dead so that His Church might have life. This ultimate act of cleaving reveals the depth of God's love—a love that transforms, redeems, and unites us to Him forever.

This mutual relationship, however, is fragile. When the unity between Man and Life is disrupted, the consequences reverberate far beyond the individual, affecting the collective purpose and identity of God's people. Life's disobedience serves as a sobering reminder of the spiritual death that follows separation from God's will.

Life's Disobedience Causes Us to Rethink Death

With a deeper understanding of Life's role, we might reconsider the belief that physical death entered the world solely due to the first man's sin. In Scripture and tradition, death often signifies separation from God rather than merely physical mortality. We do not die purely because of Man—or allegorically, Jacob—but because, as mortal beings naturally inclined toward human passions, we experience spiritual death when we stray from God's guidance, and obedience turns to disobedience.

The primary message of the creation and Fall allegories is this spiritual truth about life and death, intended to guide followers of "the way." Reading these narratives as explanations for physical death alone can obscure the deeper spiritual realities they address. Instead, it is essential to approach biblical references to death and resurrection without presuming they refer exclusively to the physical body.

St. Gregory of Nyssa, in *On the Soul and Resurrection* (1993), provides insight into this concept:

> Thus Paul, advising those who were able to hear him to lay hold on perfection, indicates also the mode in which they may attain that object, telling them that they must "put off the old man," and put on the man "which is renewed after the image of Him that created him."

St. Gregory encourages us to see resurrection as an ongoing spiritual transformation, beginning when we turn away from sin and toward God. If resurrection begins in this life, it means we are awakening from spiritual death—a separation from God.

In order to understand the nature of the death introduced by Man and Life, we must first understand a fundamental truth—immortality belongs to God alone:

1 Timothy 6:15b–16a

15b To him who is the blessed and only Ruler, the King of kings, and Lord of lords,

16a alone possessing immortality and dwelling in unapproachable light.

A common misconception is that humanity began as immortal beings who later became subject to death. However, a different interpretation emerges when we consider the story of Adam and Eve as a metaphor for the collective identity of humanity, particularly representing Moses and the children of Israel—the first nation chosen to embody God's image.

In this view, God selected a people who were already mortal. The concept of spiritual death was introduced when the people of Israel, symbolized by Eve or Life, chose disobedience over obedience, and thus converted herself into Death. This act severed their unity with the Divine—the sole source of immortality and eternal life.

This separation symbolizes humanity's collective departure from divine guidance. The consequence of this estrangement is a life bereft of God's presence, reflecting how spiritual death, rather than physical death, entered human existence. St. Paul affirms that "death reigned" even before the Law was given.[61]

Yet when God encountered Jacob in the wilderness, He provided Jacob and his descendants a path of transformation. Though they remained mortal, as they had always been, God offered them eternal life as a journey—marked by obedience and inner stillness—that allowed them to dwell in His eternal presence.

---

[61] Romans 5:14

This understanding does not diminish the promise of physical resurrection and eternal life secured by Christ. Rather, it urges us to embrace spiritual resurrection now, rising from sin and growing into God's likeness. If we focus only on the final reward, we risk overlooking the transformative work of renewal and resurrection to which we are called in this life.

Summarizing Life's Significance

The story of Man and Life is a profound allegory that encapsulates humanity's journey through salvation history and illustrates the connections between Moses and the nation of Israel, as well as between Christ and the Church. Understanding these figures as symbolic instead of merely historical reveals deep insights that enrich our Scriptural interpretation. Life represents not only the first woman but also the collective identity of God's people, who are called to live in obedience and faith.

Through Christ, the "last Man," we are offered redemption and the opportunity to become living tabernacles of the Holy Spirit. As we conform to His image and uphold tradition, we actively participate in restoring creation and fulfilling God's redemptive plan.

As we reflect on the allegory of Man and Life, we are reminded of the ongoing call to obedience and unity. Just as Life depended on Man for her purpose and identity, so too must we, as God's people, cleave to obedience while He faithfully cleaves to us. His sacrifice restores and sustains us, and in this unity, we discover the true meaning of life—one that is lived in God's presence and continually transformed by His grace.

Chapter Eighteen

The Serpent

In our exploration of biblical allegory, we now turn our attention to the enigmatic figure of the serpent. Having examined the symbolic roles of Man and Life, we delve into the narratives that shape the serpent's imagery and intentions. This chapter uncovers the serpent's allegorical roots by analyzing two key stories: King Nahash's interaction with Jabesh-Gilead and Balaam's encounter with his donkey.

Through linguistic connections, symbolic interpretations, and the concept of adversarial roles in Scripture, we'll uncover deeper spiritual truths about temptation, obedience, and the nature of opposition to God's will. As we explore these stories, we continue to uncover patterns of spiritual opposition that pervade Israel's history, illuminating how, just as Man and Life faced a deceiver in Eden, the children of Israel encountered adversarial forces seeking to disrupt their divine allegiance.

This analysis not only enriches our understanding of the Fall narrative but also reveals recurring themes of spiritual conflict throughout Scripture.

The Serpent's Allegorical Roots

We will now step outside the Law and delve into the first book of Samuel for the first source of the serpent's inspiration. I remind the reader that I approach this from the perspective that the creation and Fall allegories were written many centuries after

Moses. Therefore, drawing connections from Samuel's account is valid within this context.

Before examining the passage, it's important to understand the background: the people of Israel had demanded a king, which God viewed as a rejection of His rule.[62] Though God initially resisted, He relented and had Samuel anoint Saul as king. Soon after, the Ammonite king, Nahash, besieged Jabesh-Gilead, where, in desperation, the men of the community sought a treaty. Nahash agreed but only on the cruel condition that they allow him to gouge out their right eye:

1 Samuel 11:1–2

1 Then Nahash the Ammonite came up, and encamped against Jabesh-gilead; and all the men of Jabesh said unto Nahash: "Make a covenant with us, and we will serve thee."

2 And Nahash the Ammonite said unto them: "On this condition will I make it with you, that all your right eyes be put out; and I will lay it for a reproach upon all Israel."

King Nahash: A Serpentine Adversary

It is remarkable that so few have connected King Nahash to the serpent in Genesis, as *nakhash* (נחש, nah-KHAHSH) means "serpent"—the same word used in the Genesis account. While this connection remains speculative, and the serpent's ultimate inspiration can never be certain, the linguistic and thematic parallels are intriguing enough to warrant reflection. Both stories center on deception and disarmament, suggesting a deliberate connection.

---

[62] 1 Samuel 10:18–19

Linguistic Connections: Nakhash and Yabashah

Beyond *nakhash*, another significant Hebrew word deepens this theme: *yabashah* (יבשה, yah-bah-SHAH), meaning "dry land." As explored in the chapter "Separating the Dry Land," this term consistently refers to places of safety from surrounding chaotic waters—whether literal or symbolic.

This connection becomes even more intriguing when we examine the town of Jabesh-Gilead. The name *Jabesh* derives from *yavesh* (יבש, yah-VEYSH), meaning "dry," and shares the same root as *yabashah*. Such a detail might seem incidental, but the parallel is compelling: Jabesh, situated in the mountainous region of Gilead, evokes the idea of dry land—a place of refuge amid chaos.

Symbolic Significance: False Refuge and Deception

Herein lies the symbolic significance: King Nahash's offer of safety to the men of Jabesh may symbolize a counterfeit attempt to imitate God's role as the true provider of refuge. Throughout Scripture, dry land consistently represents salvation and divine deliverance—seen in Noah's ark finding rest, the passage through the Red Sea by the children of Israel, their safe journey through the wilderness, and even Jonah's deliverance onto dry ground. In contrast, Nahash's offer, veiled in deceptive generosity, reflects a false salvation—an inversion of God's genuine deliverance and protection.

While this connection remains interpretive, it underscores the recurring biblical themes of chaos, refuge, and deception. Such linguistic and symbolic insights invite us to see beyond the surface of the text, revealing layers of meaning that enrich our understanding of Scripture's allegorical depth.

Adversarial Roles in Biblical Allegory

The parallels between Nahash and the serpent in Genesis are striking: Nahash represents a ruler who seeks to sever Israel's loyalty to God and redirect it toward himself, much like the serpent sought to supplant Man and Life's obedience with allegiance to his deceitful counsel. Both figures challenge divine authority, seeking to draw followers away from God's protective guidance.

Nahash's demand to gouge out the right eye has an interesting symbolic meaning. The right eye is critical in battle because most people are right-handed, and it signifies the ability to resist oppression offensively. Blinding it would render the men defenseless and dependent on King Nahash. Similarly, the serpent in Eden aimed to spiritually disarm Man and Life, turning them from God and leaving them exposed to spiritual danger, unable to exercise vigilance and defense against their inner enemies.

This theme of vigilance against adversarial forces—be they thoughts, passions, or deceptive influences—runs throughout Scripture. Just as King Nahash and the serpent in Eden represent forces that disarm and separate humanity from God, we encounter another striking example in the story of Balaam and his donkey.

However, in this next example, the adversarial role takes on a surprising form: a talking she-ass who, unlike the serpent of Eden, becomes an instrument of truth rather than deception. This narrative reveals an interesting dimension of spiritual adversaries in Jewish storytelling: they serve not only to challenge but to illuminate deeper truths about obedience, perception, and God's will.

Balaam's Donkey: An Unexpected Adversary

Balaam provides yet another inspiration for *The Fall of Man* allegory. This involves two key episodes.

In the first episode, the Moabite king Balak fears becoming one of Israel's conquered lands after seeing their numbers and learning of their victory over the Amorites. He sends messengers to the prophet Balaam, requesting that he come to Balak and curse the Israelites so that they may not prevail against the Moabites. Balaam refuses, but after a second visit from the messengers, he agrees to go with them to see the king.

Balaam is riding on a she-ass, which miraculously sees an angel guarding the narrow passage through which they are traveling. When she stops and refuses to proceed, Balaam begins to strike her. Despite this, she refuses to proceed and even lies down underneath Balaam, leading him to beat her even more. According to the story, God opens her mouth, and she has a brief conversation with Balaam in which she asks him why he is behaving in this manner. God opens Balaam's eyes so that he, too, can see the angel standing in the way. He acknowledges his error and offers to turn back, but the angel permits him to continue on his journey to see King Balak. Despite all the king's coercions, Balaam refuses to curse the people of Israel, and he returns to his home.

In the second episode, we learn only briefly that Balaam, who once followed God's will by not cursing Israel, later leads the Israelites into idolatry with the Moabite women:

Numbers 31:16

16 Behold, these caused the children of Israel, through the counsel of Balaam, to revolt so as to break faith with the Lord in the matter of Peor.

These stories lead us to discover a concept that underpins both the Genesis and Balaam narratives: the role of an adversary in Jewish storytelling as a tool for revealing deeper truths and guiding God's people.

The Multifaceted Role of Adversaries

On the surface, the connection between *The Parable of Balaam* and *The Fall of Man* might not be immediately apparent. In other words, it might not be clear how one inspired the other. However, a closer look at the key motifs and Hebrew terms shared between the two reveals layers of meaning that link these narratives in an entirely logical way. Let's delve into these connections. The first connection is in the term "adversary:"

Numbers 22:22

22 And God's anger was kindled because he went, and the angel of the Lord placed himself in the way for an ***adversary*** against him. Now he was riding upon his ass, and his two servants were with him.

What the translation obscures here is that the Hebrew word for "adversary" is the same word that is usually translated elsewhere as the proper name "Satan."

Satan: Beyond the Personal Name

The Hebrew word *satan* (שטן, sah-TAHN) means "adversary," and in the Balaam narrative, the angel assumes this role by blocking Balaam's path to King Balak. The she-ass refuses to move and effectively joins the angel as a co-adversary in opposing Balaam's journey. This contrasts with the serpent in *The Fall of Man*, where the adversarial role is fulfilled by tempting Life to defy God. In both cases, the talking animal functions in the same role but with opposing intentions—one to prevent disobedience, the other to encourage it.

It's crucial to understand that the Hebrew word *satan* is never a personal name but a description of a role in which one being opposes another. This concept is neutral in itself, indicating only opposition, not necessarily evil intent. Unfortunately, many translations have rendered it as "Satan," treating it as a personal name, which has historically been inferred by most to refer to a singular evil being. Instead, when this word appears in the Bible, it is best read as "adversary." Context alone should tell us whether that role serves a righteous or evil purpose.

Talking Animals: Messengers of Spiritual Truth

We must recognize that the talking animals in these narratives are not literal characters but carefully crafted narrative devices. Their role is to illuminate deeper spiritual truths and reinforce the symbolic framework of each story. Within the biblical allegory, these creatures serve as messengers—not of spoken words in a literal sense but of the conflicts, choices, and divine instructions woven into the text. Through their "speech," these animals reveal the inner struggles and decisions that shape human interaction with the sacred.

Natural Passions: Tools for Obedience or Rebellion

The decision to use animals in adversarial roles is not whimsical by any means. From a hesychastic perspective and reading of the Scriptures, beasts represent our natural passions. The contrast between the serpent's adversarial role and the donkey's resistance highlights a key insight: the traits that emerge from our natural passions can either assist us in obeying God or lead us astray. As Evagrius Ponticus, a Desert Father, wrote in *The Praktikos & Chapters On Prayer* (2022):

> The nature of indignation is to fight the demons and to struggle for any sort of pleasure. For this reason the angels suggest to us spiritual pleasures and the blessedness [coming] from them; they encourage us to direct our anger towards the demons. The latter, however, dragging us towards worldly desires, violently

> force our indignation against nature to fight human beings, so as to darken the nous, separating it from Knowledge, and [thus] making it a traitor to the virtues.

In this light, the talking animals embody these choices, symbolizing how our natural passions can be directed constructively or destructively. The donkey's refusal to proceed represents the transformation of our natural impulses from stubbornness and rebellion into restraint and obedience. The serpent's speech, on the other hand, suggests how these same natural inclinations, when unchecked, lead to the self-indulgence of one's own willfulness, which leads to disobedience.

The Implausibility of Animals Speaking

On a practical level, the notion of animals speaking—especially in the complex phonetics of Hebrew—presents a physical impossibility. Languages require precise combinations of tongue movements, cheek muscle development, and intricate lip and jaw formations to articulate specific sounds. In Semitic languages, many sounds, including guttural, velar, dental, labial, and sibilant articulations, rely heavily on the human palate, tongue, and throat muscles. These animals, whether a donkey or a serpent, lack the anatomical structures necessary to produce such a sophisticated range of sounds, particularly the glottal and pharyngeal movements integral to Semitic phonology.

Rethinking the Literal Interpretation

The only plausible explanation for them speaking a Semitic language would involve an external entity manipulating them, akin to using a ventriloquist's dummy. This interpretation challenges plausibility and prompts us to reconsider the literalist's grasp of this parable. The physical impossibility of animal speech highlights the narrative's symbolic intent. Naturally, animals lack the capacity for human language, which reinforces their allegorical role and encourages readers to see the characters' "speech" as representing spiritual truths rather than literal conversation.

These animals act as living metaphors, capturing our attention through their vivid imagery. They embody roles of opposition or guidance, ultimately serving the allegory's message. By attributing speech to them, the biblical narrative deepens the story by allowing us to explore the dynamics of listening to divine guidance and either leveraging our natural passions in His service or opposing Him in those moments of temptation when we face choices.

Postures of Faithfulness and Defiance

Another meaningful connection in the story of Balaam lies in the donkey's posture, which carries symbolic weight in relation to obedience and submission. When the donkey sees the angel, she lies down under Balaam:

Numbers 22:27

27 And the ass saw the angel of the Lord, and ***she lay down*** under Balaam, and Balaam's anger was kindled, and he smote the ass with his staff.

The Hebrew word *rabatz* (רבץ, rah-VAHTS), translated as "she lay down," suggests a posture of prostration and submission to the divine will. This term also appears in Genesis 4:7, where God warns Cain that "sin ***crouches*** at the door," demonstrating how *rabatz* can signify obedience or deception, depending on intent. Here, the story of Cain and his offering serves to illustrate the dual implications of both this term and the position of prostration.

Our primary focus, however, is on the contrast between the donkey in Balaam's story and the serpent in Eden. Similar postures can reflect either spiritual alignment or opposition. The donkey's voluntary prostration as it lies on its belly embodies obedience to divine guidance, while the serpent's curse to crawl on its belly is a consequence of its defiance. Together, these stances convey that one's posture—both literal and figurative—can indicate faithfulness or rebellion, mirroring the dual nature of an adversarial role: we can either resist sin or resist rebellion. The choice is ours!

Lessons from Adversarial Figures

The narratives of King Nahash and Balaam's she-ass illuminate the multifaceted role of adversarial figures in biblical allegory, showcasing how themes of disarmament, deception, and divine confrontation permeate Israel's spiritual history. By examining the serpent's imagery through these stories, we uncover important lessons about the interplay between human will, natural passions, and divine guidance.

Whether through Nahash's attempt to mimic God's provision or the she-ass's transformation of stubbornness into obedience, these adversarial characters reveal the choices we face in directing our passions toward either faithfulness or defiance. Together, these stories underscore the constant struggle to remain vigilant, discerning, and aligned with God's will amidst the chaos of temptation and opposition.

Part Six

Finding Our Way Back

If the Bible's ultimate purpose is the transformation of the soul—leading to inner stillness and divine communion—then practical methods for achieving this transformation must exist. While the Scriptures may not lay out detailed instructions, Eastern Orthodox Christianity has uniquely preserved these practices, faithfully passing them down through the generations.

As we embark on this series of chapters, we will begin by briefly exploring how the Church's liturgical services guide us along the path of purification and stillness. These services help us to reflect God's image and draw near to His presence, symbolically regaining the Garden of Eden. These services represent the most basic path for leading the soul back to God's presence.

Next, we will examine foundational aspects of the Jesus Prayer that are often overlooked, such as the deeper significance of the name of Jesus and the true aim of the practice. We will also address the obstacles this spiritual work encounters, offering insights from the sages who have counseled believers on overcoming these challenges.

Building on this foundation, we will explore "advanced" practices tailored for those who may find the pursuit of continuous prayer challenging in the context of daily life. These supplemental techniques, while not entirely original except in their framing, aim to contribute meaningfully to the ongoing dialogue on hesychasm.

Chapter Nineteen

Liturgy as an Act of Creation

Tilling the Soil

Eastern Orthodox Christianity offers a rich tapestry of spiritual tools designed to guide believers back to God. At the heart of these practices lies the Divine Liturgy, a profound spiritual exercise that can be likened to cultivating one's soul. This comparison between spiritual growth and agricultural nurturing is not merely poetic; it is deeply rooted in the linguistic and theological foundations of the faith.

The Synonymous Meaning of Tilling and Liturgy

The Hebrew word for "till," *avad* (עבד, ah-VAHD), reveals layers of meaning that extend beyond the physical work involved in cultivating the land. By examining this term, we uncover how tilling serves as a metaphor for spiritual practice, preparing our hearts to encounter God. In the Hebrew Bible, the verb *avad* and its noun cognate *avodah* (עבדה, ah-voh-DAH) appear numerous times, carrying a variety of meanings. However, we are only interested in the contexts that reveal its dual meaning of "service and worship." We see this implied meaning when these terms are used to describe service in attending to the Tabernacle.[63]

---

[63] Exodus 38:21; Numbers 4:24, 27–28, 33; 7:5, 7–8; 8:22, 25; 16:9; 18:4,6–7, 21, 23, 31; 1 Chronicles 6:32, 48; 9:13, 19, 28; 23:26, 28; 24:3, 19; 28:13, 20–21; 2 Chronicles 8:14; 31:2, 16; 35:10, 15–16

In the thirty-five cases mentioned in the footnote, the Greek equivalent, identifiable by comparing the Septuagint with the Hebrew Bible, is *leitourgia* (*λειτουργία*, lee-toor-YEE-ah), from which we get the word "liturgy." This linguistic connection illustrates the parallel between the physical act of tilling the ground and spiritual cultivation. Liturgy originally referred to public service or works performed for the community, aligning with the Hebrew concept of *avad* as encompassing both worship of God and service to others.

These connections are illustrated in the Genesis narrative of Man and Life's expulsion from Eden. After they were cast out of the Garden, God commanded them to cultivate (*avad*) the ground, which was now burdened with thorns and thistles. These weeds were not placed there by God but were the natural consequence of Life (Eve) having sown the pernicious seeds of doubt that led to disobedience.

Seen through this lens, it becomes clear that God's directive was not merely about cultivating the earth; rather it was a metaphorical call to engage in spiritual practices to reclaim paradise. The "ground" Man and Life were commanded to till was not the physical soil but the inner ground of their souls.

Tilling: Not a Punishment But a Way Back to God

Man and Life's task, then, was to discern and uproot the thorns of destructive thoughts and the thistles of harmful emotions that threatened to choke out the virtues within their souls. The thorns and thistles were not imposed as a punishment for humanity's rebellion; rather they were planted there by man himself, who had sown the seeds of doubt within the inner landscape of his soul.

This viewpoint also addresses a common challenge to a literal interpretation of the Creation story: If God made everything in six days, why did the thorns only emerge after Man's fall? The explanation is twofold: the text refers not to physical creation but rather to a spiritual reality, and the thorns symbolize the internal obstacles we cultivate in our souls when we start to question the traditions passed down, which was exactly Life's sin that caused her to assume the role of deciding what is good and evil.

Tilling as Restoration

The way we view this episode in Man and Life's narrative comes down to perspective. Do we see God as an angry, offended deity seeking opportunities to judge and condemn humanity, or do we recognize a God who lovingly works to restore us to Him? While a literal interpretation of Genesis may emphasize punishment, the allegorical view reveals a God who gently guides humanity through spiritual cultivation. This aligns with the Eastern Orthodox understanding of the Church as the "hospital of the soul," where healing and restoration are at the forefront of God's relationship with humanity.

The command to "till the ground" can be understood as a compassionate call that continues today, inviting us to cultivate the soil of our hearts. Through this ongoing work, we become prepared to receive the life-giving rain of His presence. Just as Man and Life were tasked with tilling the inner ground of their souls, the Church provides us with the liturgical rhythm of Orthros and the Divine Liturgy to guide our spiritual cultivation. These services serve as acts of healing, renewing our souls and preparing us for communion with God.

In this sense, the liturgical services of the Church can be seen as participating in the act of creation itself. Though it is not traditional liturgical theology to compare these services to the Creation narrative, this perspective does not conflict with the Church's teachings. On the contrary, it highlights the Church's role in guiding us toward the restoration and renewal that God has desired for humanity since the beginning. The parallels between these liturgical acts and the act of creation in Genesis will be explored further in the following discussion.

Orthros: Preparing the Soil of the Soul

For those who regularly attend the Divine Liturgy, a deliberate pattern begins to emerge: The sequence of worship steadily builds toward participation in the Eucharist. This preparation begins the moment we enter the parish doors. As we step inside, we leave behind the distractions of the world, mirroring the gathering of dry land from the chaotic waters in Genesis. Just as God created the sacred ground for the children of Israel, free from idolatrous influences, we too enter a space set apart—a holy ground where we begin to attune our hearts to His presence.

Orthros, the morning prayer service, continues this preparation by laying the spiritual foundation for worship. Through hymns and doxologies, the service exalts God, reminding the faithful of His majesty and inviting them to approach the light of His presence with reverence.

During this service, we follow along with the reading of the great Psalm of Repentance,[64] applying its words to our own lives, acknowledging our uncleanness, and offering the acceptable sacrifice of contrition. This moment can be understood as a spiritual "separation of light from darkness," where we lay aside our sin, turning from the darkness to seek God's light.

Orthros thus softens the soil of the heart, preparing it to receive the nourishing rain of God's presence during the Divine Liturgy. It is a time of turning, repentance, and spiritual readiness, ensuring that we approach the Eucharist with a heart attuned to Christ's presence and open to His transformative work.

---

[64] Psalm 51

The Divine Liturgy: Completing the Creation

The Divine Liturgy builds upon the cultivating work of Orthros and guides us toward communion with God. By His grace, we are made holy, worthy, and transformed into His likeness through worship, prayer, and active participation in the Liturgy. The climax of the Divine Liturgy—the Eucharist—provides a foretaste of the eternal rest and joy of the Kingdom of God.

In this divine mystery, we come into communion with God and one another as the Bride united with the Bridegroom. As the Bride of Christ, the Church embodies a restored Eve (Life), united with the "last Adam (Man),"[65] Christ Jesus, through obedience and life. This transformation reverses the disobedience and spiritual death brought by the first Eve. In doing so, we are united with Him and once again experience the Garden of Eden, partaking of the Tree of Life.

This progression unveils a profound connection between the Divine Liturgy and the Creation allegory. Each liturgical stage mirrors God's creative acts: separating the light of obedience from the darkness of disobedience, entering a sacred space of order as we leave a chaotic world behind, embracing unity as we disengage from our individual lives, and, ultimately, guiding the Body of Christ as one into divine rest. Just as God shaped the cosmos through distinct creative phases, the liturgy shapes the spiritual journey of the faithful, transforming their inner world from chaos to divine order.

Skipping these preparatory steps and showing up just in time for the Eucharist not only disturbs the deep worship and contemplation in which others are engaged but also overlooks the complete transformative power only found by participating in both the combined Orthros and Divine Liturgy. If we do not participate in

---

[65] 1 Corinthians 15:45

the entire spiritual journey, we may arrive unprepared, much like a guest without the appropriate wedding garment.

Just as tilling is essential before harvest, worshipers are encouraged to immerse themselves in the preparatory elements of the Liturgy. Neglecting this spiritual effort lessens worship's transformative essence. It is through the uniting of Orthros and the Divine Liturgy that we prepare to approach the Eucharist with gratitude, joy, and reverence, entering into complete communion with God.

Together, these services provide Orthodox Christians with a foundational path to grow closer to Christ and be conformed to His image. For those seeking to enhance this journey of purification and illumination, the Church also offers the personal practice of the Jesus Prayer, which we will explore next.

Chapter Twenty

Resetting Expectations of the Jesus Prayer

It was our Lord who taught us the importance of a prayer that pleads for mercy. In *The Parable of the Publican and the Pharisee*, Jesus extols the humility of the publican:

Luke 18:13b–14a

13b . . . God, be merciful to me, a sinner!

14a I tell you, this man, rather than the
other, went down to his house
justified . . .

Later, in the same chapter, Jesus heals a blind man who comes pleading, "Jesus, son of David, have mercy on me."[66] This prayer has evolved over the centuries into its present form. We will start by exploring the practice of reciting the Jesus Prayer in its most basic form.

Entering the Practice

For many Eastern Orthodox Christians, the Jesus Prayer is a familiar and cherished spiritual discipline. However, for those encountering it for the first time, a brief introduction is valuable. The prayer is typically synchronized with the breath to create a rhythm of focus and stillness:

---

[66] Luke 18:38

Inhale	Lord Jesus Christ, Son of God . . .
Exhale	Have mercy upon me, a sinner.

This foundational approach integrates the mind and heart in a rhythmic pattern that promotes inner peace and attentiveness. To aid in this practice, a *komboskini* (prayer rope) is often used, featuring a varying number of knots, typically ranging from thirty-three to over three hundred. With each cycle of inhalation and exhalation, the practitioner moves their fingers along one knot, repeating the prayer until the entire prayer rope—or a desired portion—is completed. This tactile element helps the practitioner maintain focus, deepening their connection to the prayer.

Since the supplicant is invoking the name of Jesus, it is worth exploring what is meant by the "name" of our Lord.

The Name of Jesus

As we begin, it is crucial to reflect on the name of Jesus—the very essence of the Jesus Prayer. Too often, we engage in this sacred practice without fully understanding or appreciating what or who we are truly invoking. Some mistakenly believe that simply pronouncing the syllables of His name is sufficient to drive away inner demons. But is this belief accurate? Does the name itself carry a mystical power in its sounds? And if so, does this power extend to all variations and translations of His name, or is it confined to the original language in which He was named? These are both valid and important questions.

If the power resides in the letters, syllables, and sounds then it would seem necessary to return to the original Aramaic (*Yeshua*) or Hebrew (*Yehoshua*), as these were the names spoken during His earthly life and the name that the angel Gabriel commanded Mary to give her Son. Given that "Jesus" is a Greek-to-Latin transliteration, it cannot possess any inherent mystical power simply by virtue of its phonetics. Instead, we must consider this: does the power of His name reside in its audible form, or does it come from what the name represents?

To understand the true significance of invoking His name, we must examine how the concept of "name" is presented in the Hebrew Bible. In Scripture, a name represents much more than just a label; it symbolizes authority, power, presence, and reputation. For instance, in 1 Samuel 17:45, David declares, "I come to thee in the name of the Lord of hosts," invoking the authority and power of God. In Proverbs 22:1, we read, "A good name is rather to be chosen than great riches," where "name" symbolizes reputation. Similarly, in Deuteronomy 12:11, Moses speaks of the place thus: "the Lord your God shall choose to cause His name to dwell there," signifying God's presence among His people.

This profoundly shapes how we approach the Jesus Prayer. Invoking His name is not about mechanical repetition or the phonetics of the word. Rather, it is about invoking His presence through faith, humility, and stillness. If we repeat His name thousands of times, moving endlessly around our prayer rope, but fail to enter His presence, what have we truly achieved? The real purpose of the Jesus Prayer is not in the sounds of the name but in aligning ourselves with Christ, opening our hearts to His transforming presence, and deepening our communion with Him.

Not only must we remember this understanding while practicing the Jesus Prayer, but we also need to recognize our goals through its continual repetition.

Clarifying the Goal of the Jesus Prayer

Generally, within Eastern Orthodoxy, we are taught that the goal is to achieve a state where the Jesus Prayer adheres to St. Paul's call to "pray without ceasing." Yet, this demands a deeper understanding of the apostle's intent behind this phrase. We will explore how early Christians understood the concept of unceasing prayer in their spiritual lives. Without this insight, our efforts might lead us to pursue a goal that is unrealistic for the layperson. Worse yet, if we have an incorrect understanding of its goal, we may become discouraged from even entering these waters.

Continuous or Continual?

A widely held belief is that the purpose of this prayer is to reach a point where the Jesus Prayer repeats itself in our minds. Many understand the goal to be a state where the prayer becomes continuous and ever-present. But the question that faces us is, "Did St. Paul mean 'continuous' or 'continual'?" The difference is substantial and of great importance to us.

The Continuous View

In the book, *The Art of Prayer: An Orthodox Anthology* (1966), St. Theophan the Recluse describes how the Jesus Prayer progresses from being initially continual to eventually becoming continuous:

> We do not need any special help from God in order to begin the work of repeating this prayer in the morning, in the evening, walking, sitting, lying down, working, or at leisure. By being always active in this way we can of ourselves train the tongue to repeat the Prayer even without conscious effort.

This view suggests that, with persistent effort, the Jesus Prayer can become a continuous undercurrent in one's thoughts—a state of unbroken communion with God. However, for laypeople, this ideal may seem unattainable. How can one achieve such constancy amid the demands of work, family, and everyday life?

Rather than dismissing this goal as unrealistic, let us first consider what St. Paul meant by "pray without ceasing."

St. Paul's Understanding of "Without Ceasing"

The phrase just referred to is found in 1 Thessalonians 5:17 and is often cited as support for the goal of continuous prayer. To see if this understanding is correct, we must examine the Greek word *adialeiptos* (*ἀδιαλείπτως*, ah-thee-ah-LEEP-tos), which is used in the cited verse. Does it mean prayer that never stops (without ceasing) or prayer that recurs at regular intervals?

Thankfully, St. Paul, in his epistle to the Romans, provides that answer:

Romans 1:9

> 9 God is my witness, whom I serve with my spirit in the gospel of His Son, that ***without ceasing*** I mention you always in my prayers.

Here, St. Paul describes his prayers for the Roman believers using the same Greek word found in 1 Thessalonians 5:17. Yet, it is evident that he is not praying for them every second; rather they are among the many for whom he prays regularly. We know this because he tells the Ephesians[67] and Philippians[68] the exact same thing!

This inherently implies that his prayers for the Romans are continual rather than continuous. If we are to quote Paul's exhortation to "pray without ceasing," we must also embrace his understanding and use of the term. We thereby allow Scripture to interpret itself, and we let the author of those words explain to us what he meant and how he used the term in other contexts.

This perspective suggests that the goal of the Jesus Prayer should not be to function like an endlessly looping song stuck in our

---

[67] Ephesians 1:16

[68] Philippians 1:3

minds as an earworm. Instead, the Jesus Prayer is a sacred tool for achieving a purified heart and mind—free from both good and bad thoughts and images—leading to inner stillness and the knowledge of God.

I do not question the ability of some individuals to reach a state where the Jesus Prayer repeats continuously in their hearts. However, this book's primary audience is the layperson. For that reason, I will set aside the goal of "continuous" prayer and propose alternative objectives that may be equally, if not more, beneficial for both laypeople and monastics. As bold as that may sound, I leave it to the reader to evaluate these methods once they are presented.

True spiritual growth, however, requires more than simply overlaying a repetitive prayer onto the unresolved noise of our thoughts and passions. Much like the old tape-recording system that uses an eraser head to remove previous recordings before laying down new music, we, too, must simultaneously erase the inner noise that clutters our soul. This is a necessary step in the transformative process, ensuring that what follows is clear, pure, and enduring.

We need to address this noise to understand what we're trying to eliminate and how it disrupts our peace. Without recognizing how our own thoughts challenge our practice of the Jesus Prayer, we cannot formulate a strategy to take control of our inner landscape.

Chapter Twenty-One

Obstacles to the Jesus Prayer

Is the Jesus Prayer Enough?

During my practice of the Jesus Prayer, I found that it, or admittedly perhaps I, was not completely successful in keeping out unwanted "noise," thus thwarting my efforts to gain a purified mind focused on God. Having briefly practiced Zen a couple of decades before entering the ancient faith, I had developed an awareness of the thoughts and feelings that continuously arise within a person's consciousness.

Through this acquired awareness, I came to understand why the Jesus Prayer alone wasn't enough for me. While the repetition of the prayer successfully engaged one part of my mind, it left other cognitive functions unoccupied. Although I couldn't fully articulate the scientific reasoning behind this at the time, I intuitively sensed that my observations were valid. I believed that with some research, I could uncover insights—both for myself and others—that might explain the underlying phenomena.

As I wrestled with this challenge, I learned that our minds are wired to process multiple stimuli simultaneously. Neuroscience reveals that while Broca's area in the brain processes language, other parts, like the visual cortex, can still generate mental images. This explains why distractions arise during prayer, as our minds naturally try to process multiple channels of stimuli at once. Even rapid or focused repetition of the prayer might not be enough to block out these parallel intrusive images.

These images can invade and dominate the mind. Similar to watching a muted television screen, where the brain tries to create an accompanying narrative for the silent images, our mind instinctively seeks to explain or expand on visual images that arise from within. This mental process can overpower the language-focused effort of the Jesus Prayer, relegating it to little more than background elevator music.

Bullying Images

In essence, the visual cortex can "bully" Broca's area, forcing it into submission and interrupting prayer with its own "movie" playing in the mind's theater. This suggests that a more integrated approach, one that acknowledges the role of visual imagery and works with it, may be necessary to overcome distractions.

To resolve this dilemma, we should not view the visual cortex as the enemy of our intent. Rather than letting internal images disrupt our attempts, we can turn them into allies—subservient to us rather than being our masters. In the process I outline below, my intent is not to quash internal images but to use them as launchpads into higher awareness.

Before explaining this process, it's important to explore how the sages of our faith attempted to address similar distractions that they encountered in their spiritual practices.

The Sages Address The Distractions

While the Jesus Prayer, when practiced continually, brings immense spiritual benefits, it is clear that repetition alone may not fully address the deeper challenges we face in maintaining focus and stillness. Many practitioners, both past and present, have encountered distractions—unresolved thoughts and feelings that emerge during prayer despite their best efforts.

Recognizing these challenges, the sages of the *Philokalia* and other Orthodox texts did not settle for a singular prayer method. Instead, they developed various techniques and approaches to tackle the mind's complexity and keep distractions at bay. These methods offer valuable insight into how we can enrich our practice and address the obstacles. Each method is appropriate at some stage, but eventually, the practitioner will outgrow them and need improved methods to complement the Jesus Prayer.

Fast or Slow Prayer?

Even within the *Philokalia*, we find different approaches presented, indicating that perhaps what works for one person may not work for another. Alternatively, an explanation may be that what works at one stage of our practice may not work in the next stage.

St. Gregory of Sinai, in the *Philokalia, Vol. 4* (Palmer, 2024), presents one approach for the beginner:

> In the case of a beginner in the art of spiritual warfare . . . when thoughts invade you, in place of weapons call on the Lord Jesus frequently and persistently and then they will retreat.

In the *Philokalia, Vol.4* (Palmer, 2024), we are advised that St. Symeon the New Theologian, in *The Three Methods*, advocates for a slow, more focused approach to prayer:

> . . . secondly, control over the breathing so that its pace is slowed down; thirdly, inner exploration by the intellect, which searches for the place of the heart. All of this, so it seems, is meant to precede rather than to accompany the recitation of the Jesus Prayer;

As St. Gregory of Sinai advises, a faster pace may overwhelm the mind's ability to get distracted. At the same time, St. Symeon the New Theologian's slower approach allows one to savor each word, perhaps leading to deeper penetration of the prayer into the heart.

There are still other saints who recognized the problem I described above regarding the interrupting images of the visual cortex and sought to address the issue.

Visualizing Weapons to Fight Unwanted Thoughts

St. Diodochos of Photiki and St. John of Karpathos recommend engaging the mind's visual components to support one's spiritual efforts. Their advice clearly shows that they understood the challenge of wandering thoughts and engaged the visual cortex to enhance focus during prayer.

St. Diodochos of Photiki, in the *Philokalia, Vol. 1* (Palmer, 2024), writes as follows:

> If the intellect at that time cleaves fervently to the remembrance of the glorious and holy name of the Lord Jesus and uses it as a weapon against Satan's deception, he gives up this trick and for the future will attack the soul directly and personally.

St. John of Karpathos, also in the *Philokalia, Vol. 1* (Palmer, 2024), offers another visualization:

> A man escapes this anger by keeping his attention fixed continually within his heart during prayer, and by striving to remain within his inner sanctuary.

While somewhat effective, whether imagining the name of Jesus as a weapon or visualizing the heart as a sanctuary, I discovered these techniques do not completely quell the invading images. Simply focusing both the language and visual imagery centers of the brain toward the same goal is often inadequate. A more profound cleansing of the mind is essential for attaining genuine stillness.

Having Neither Good Nor Bad Thoughts

Some of the methods put forth by the saints in the *Philokalia* can be compared to an analogy I previously used of attempting to record over an old audio cassette. Just as older recording systems require an eraser head to clear the tape before new music can be recorded, we also must first clear the mind before anything new can be built upon it.

Erasing the Noise

Simply layering spiritual practices—such as rapid or even focused prayer recitation—on a mind full of distractions won't eliminate the underlying noise. Instead, it may result in multiple layers of inner confusion, making it more difficult to achieve mental stillness. This may lead us to give up, thinking that the practice doesn't work for us.

In hesychasm, the goal is not to drown out distractions but to cleanse the mind entirely, leaving a "clean track" where stillness can take root. As the saints of the *Philokalia* teach, this requires removing all thoughts, whether negative or seemingly positive. The mind must be freed from attachment to both good and bad thoughts if true stillness is to prevail.

The Need to Eliminate Even Positive Thoughts

While most people recognize the importance of eliminating negative thoughts, questions may emerge about why even positive thoughts should also be quieted. In the *Philokalia, Vol. 1* (Palmer, 2024), St. Symeon the New Theologian addresses this in explaining *The Three Methods*, where he declares the first two methods defective. Regarding the first method, he writes:

> When a person stands at prayer, he raises hands, eyes and intellect heavenwards, and fills his intellect with divine thoughts, with images of celestial beauty, of the angelic hosts,

> of the abodes of the righteous . . . But when someone prays in this way, without him realizing it his heart grows proud and exalted, and he regards what is happening to him as the effect of divine grace . . . Such assumptions, however, are signs of delusion, because the good is not good when it is not done in the right way . . . It will be impossible for him to attain a state of holiness or dispassion.

Here, he explains that such thoughts, though well-intentioned, can foster attachment or give rise to deluded feelings of holiness. Even genuine spiritual emotions often associated with spiritual experiences can mislead us, drawing our focus toward them rather than toward cultivating inner stillness. In the hesychastic tradition, the challenge lies in mistaking these emotions for the ultimate spiritual goal. While feelings may accompany holiness, they are not synonymous with holiness itself.

Therefore, if, during our practice, we must eliminate good and bad thoughts, as well as rising imagery, how do we do that? We accomplish this through awareness and metacognition.

Chapter Twenty-Two

From Awareness to Metacognition

Becoming Aware

True spiritual growth begins with taking full responsibility for our internal state. While we cannot control our external circumstances or the actions of others, we have complete authority over how we engage with our thoughts and feelings. This is where awareness and metacognition become critical tools for cultivating inner clarity and transformation.

By stepping beyond automatic and reactive thinking, we gain the ability to consciously observe and understand our thought processes. This practice fosters deeper self-awareness and opens the door to spiritual growth. Many people, however, live as actors in their mental dramas, playing out scripts written by automatic thinking. Rarely do they pause to ask, "Where did this thought come from?" or "Why do I feel this way?" Yet, stepping into the role of director changes everything. It enables us to observe the repetitive scripts shaping our inner lives—thoughts clinging like bubbles to a glass held in place by unresolved imperfections within us.

Through practices like the Jesus Prayer, we begin polishing the glass of our soul, loosening the grip of these clinging thoughts. By aligning our minds and breathing through prayer, we watch as these thoughts rise and disappear, gradually rewriting the script of our inner narrative. Over time, the mental movie transforms into one of clarity and intention, directed by communion with God.

An example of automatic thinking is the reliance on "scripted responses," much like an actor repeating rehearsed lines. These responses are akin to frequently used clichés that require minimal effort. We all know people who resemble pull-string dolls, repeating familiar phrases without deeper thought. Like actors in a play, they default to a conditioned response when they reach a familiar scene. This behavior reflects a lack of awareness—a failure to deliver a thoughtful, original reply.

To rise above this, we must reach a level of awareness that is closely related to the Eastern Orthodox concepts of *nepsis* (νήψις, NEEP-sees) and *diakrisis* (διάκρισις, thee-AH-kree-sees), roughly meaning "watchfulness" and "discernment," respectively. While the Church Fathers did not use the term "metacognition," which I use in the following pages, the idea aligns with what might be called "neptic discernment."

St. Isaiah the Solitary hints at this in his work *On Guarding the Intellect*, found in the *Philokalia, Vol. 1* (Palmer, 2024):

> Be attentive to yourself, so that nothing destructive can separate you from the love of God. Guard your heart, and do not grow listless and say: "How shall I guard it, since I am a sinner?"

This is a call to become the gatekeeper of all thoughts and passions that arise within us, whether from internal stirrings or external stimuli. Drawing from Orthodox traditions and personal experience, I aim to share imagery and techniques that have proven helpful in developing this practice.

While I cannot hope to surpass the profound wisdom of the saints as expressed in the *Philokalia*, it is also not my intention to present myself as someone who has achieved any notable spiritual accomplishment in life. My goal is simply to distill some of its best practices into a concise and accessible format. The *Philokalia* is a treasure trove of spiritual guidance, but its depth can be overwhelming. Those who delve into its vast teachings may find themselves struggling to extract practical takeaways for daily life. With this in mind, I hope to offer a highly condensed presentation of points that I find particularly useful. Combined with my own experiences, the insights and explanations provided here may serve as a practical guide for the reader on their spiritual journey.

Examining and Cleaning the Glass

Our thoughts and feelings often arise like carbonation bubbles in a glass of soda. Some float freely to the surface and disappear, while others cling stubbornly to the sides, held there by imperfections or leftover residue in the glass. Similarly, the recurring patterns of thoughts we experience in our inner lives are tied to unresolved flaws within us—areas of "dirt" that remain unaddressed. Each day, the same thoughts resurface, creating a mental cycle reminiscent of the monotony portrayed in the 1993 movie *Groundhog Day*. Without awareness, we remain trapped in these cycles, reliving the same stories and reactions.

Why do some thoughts drift away unnoticed, while others stick and grow into elaborate distractions? The answer lies in the imperfections of our souls. Each person's inner landscape is unique, shaped by their experiences, weaknesses, and unresolved issues. Just as bubbles cling to specific spots in a glass, thoughts attach to our vulnerabilities, forming patterns that are difficult to break.

To move beyond this cycle, we must actively "clean the glass" of our souls. Simply ignoring persistent thoughts or attempting to suppress them with sheer effort will not suffice. Nor can we rely on surface-level techniques, such as rushing through the Jesus Prayer to outpace intruding thoughts or layering new thoughts over old ones. Instead, we must address the underlying imperfections that allow these thoughts to persist.

Orthodox spirituality offers a path forward, incorporating practices of mindful repetition uniquely centered on communion with God. For example, practices like the Jesus Prayer parallel methods in other traditions, such as Zen counting exercises. In Zen, practitioners count their breaths, striving to maintain focus and noting when a thought interrupts the sequence. For many, this interruption happens quickly—sometimes before even reaching the third breath. This practice illustrates how deeply entrenched our mental habits can be and how awareness is the first step toward breaking free.

By observing our thoughts and identifying the areas where they repeatedly cling, we begin the process of cleansing our inner glass. This deliberate, prayerful effort gradually loosens the grip of recurring distractions, allowing us to cultivate stillness and clarity. Over time, the soul becomes a polished vessel, capable of reflecting God's presence and radiating inner peace.

But this work also involves stepping out of the automatic, reactive patterns that keep us trapped in the mental movies of our lives. By transitioning from actor to director, we can guide the narrative intentionally. This shift requires a methodical practice, such as the Jesus Prayer, to polish the glass of our soul and redirect our thoughts toward communion with God.

Entering the Jesus Prayer Practice

We can easily adapt this practice so that instead of counting, we repeat the Jesus Prayer, whose basic form we reviewed in the chapter "Resetting Expectations of the Jesus Prayer."

This foundational method focuses on synchronizing the prayer with our breath, engaging both the mind and the heart in a rhythmic cycle that fosters inner peace. During this practice, we will notice thoughts or images bubbling up, pulling our minds into automatic cognition. When this happens, we should not be discouraged. The very act of recognizing that we've been drawn into a narrative is a sign of progress. Thoughts are like distractions that tempt us to follow them, much like a squirrel passing before the eyes of a dog. However, through awareness and practice, we can train ourselves to let these distractions pass without engaging them.

After considerable time in this practice, we will naturally move to the following variation:

Inhale	Lord Jesus Christ, Son of God . . .
Exhale	Have mercy upon me, a sinner.
Inhale	No thoughts
Exhale	No thoughts

In case it's not obvious, we don't say "no thoughts"; we have no thoughts or images in our minds. This variation is far more advanced and presents progression toward a state where the mind is completely empty, allowing for deeper communion with God. It's important not to rush to this level of practice—it will settle upon us naturally over time as our minds become free of attachments.

To experience moments of "no thoughts," we first need to address the barriers to reaching this state. This requires a shift from being an actor in our thoughts to directly managing them, moving from automatic thinking to awareness and metacognition.

From Automatic Thinking to Metacognition

When our Jesus Prayer is interrupted by an intruding thought that begins to form a narrative, we haven't failed at all! This moment marks the transition into metacognition, the first stage of which is simple "awareness"—noticing our thoughts as they emerge without engaging with or elaborating on them. It's a straightforward acknowledgment: I see you; I know you. At this point, we become observers or watchers.

Through the lens of metacognition—the practice of observing and thinking about our own mental processes—we gain a deeper understanding of our inner world. As we attentively watch our thoughts, emotions, and mental images unfold, we begin to discern their sources and diminish their emotional impact. This transformative process reveals a profound truth: We are not our thoughts and passions. The very act of observation implies an observer—the true "self" distinct from the mental phenomena it witnesses. We are eternal beings, while thoughts and feelings are transient; therefore, they cannot be us.

One of the most potent emotional bonds tying us to our thoughts and passions is our unconscious identification with them. We often fiercely defend what we perceive as our identity, not realizing that these transient mental states do not define us.

This process often begins with the simple yet powerful act of naming our internal struggles, much as Adam named the animals in Eden, thereby establishing dominion over them. When we see a thought arise and name it, saying, "I see you, Jealousy," we objectify the emotion, allowing us to examine it with greater detachment. This naming ritual empowers us, stripping the thought or passion of its power to cling to us. By refusing to allow them to cleave unto us, we are better able to cleave unto obedience and experience life in God's presence. In doing so, we align ourselves with Christ, the Dispassionate One, striving to emulate His perfect mastery over the inner landscape of the soul.

Metacognition goes deeper, asking why a thought has arisen, what causes it to cling to us, and why it stirs certain emotions. This reflective process transforms awareness into a tool for spiritual growth, placing us fully in the role of the director of our inner theater. From this position, we take charge of the actors—our thoughts and feelings— determining where each belongs and what role it should play.

This role is also akin to that of a gardener, who decides what plants should fill the inner garden of the soul. With grace, we begin to uproot the weeds—disordered passions, anxieties, or distractions—that threaten to choke out virtue. Over time, this careful tending allows the soul to flourish, filled with the fruits of the Spirit and attuned to the stillness of God's presence.

Until we reach this point, it cannot be said we are fulfilling God's command that man should earn his bread by the sweat of his brow as he tills the ground.

Our Daily Bread

I contend the bread we earn by tilling the inner landscape of the thorns and thistles is the "daily bread" our Lord spoke of in the Lord's Prayer. We are thinking too narrowly if we believe that the bread of the Genesis narrative or the "daily bread" we pray for is the physical kind we consume, for our Lord Himself thus counseled His disciples:

Matthew 6:25–26

25 Therefore, I tell you, do not be anxious about your life, wondering what you will eat or drink; or about your body, what you will wear. Is not life more than food, and the body more than clothing?

26 See the birds of the sky: they do not sow, or reap, or gather into barns. Your heavenly Father feeds them! Are you not of much more value than they?

In light of this, how can we think that, either in this allegory or in the Lord's Prayer, He was teaching us about the procurement of our daily sustenance? In spiritual terms, bread symbolizes the presence of the Lord. This is evident in the shewbread (bread of the Presence) in the Tabernacle, a sign of God's continual presence with His people, and in the holy Eucharist, instituted at the Last Supper and celebrated to this day. By "tilling the soil"—cultivating stillness and preparing our hearts—we encounter His presence, our true daily bread.[69]

This perspective elaborates on my view in the chapter "Liturgy as an Act of Creation," where I expressed the opinion that tilling the ground was not a punishment but divine instruction guiding humanity on how to regain entrance to paradise, a process that culminates in an encounter with Christ.

This is completely in line with the teachings of the Church Fathers, for St. Augustine of Hippo wrote in *The Lord's Sermon on the Mount* (1948):

> It remains, therefore, that we should interpret "daily bread" as spiritual food, namely, the divine precepts which we are to think over and put into practice each day. It is of this that the Lord says: Labor for the food which perisheth not.

The question then is, "How do we till the ground that we may eat of our daily bread—the presence of Christ?" There are real and practical methods for accomplishing this. Tilling the soil of our hearts requires deliberate effort to confront our imperfections—those places where thoughts and emotions cling and disrupt our peace. This labor, much like polishing the soul, prepares us to encounter Christ.

Polishing the Soul and Cultivating Dispassion

We examine the thought closely, exploring its layers like a prism, until we see it clearly and remove its power. In doing so, we transform the thought into something objective, detaching it from the emotions that often give it power over us. This detachment is crucial, as it is the emotional charge that makes thoughts cling. Through this process, we cultivate the virtue exemplified by our Lord, known in Eastern Orthodoxy as the Dispassionate One. As

---

[69] John 6:35

Evagrius Ponticus wrote in *Praktikos*, "Dispassion is the flowering of the practical virtues."

If we fail to understand why certain thoughts cling to us, we will never rid ourselves of them. These unexamined areas remain fertile ground for recurring thoughts to reattach themselves. By thoroughly examining the intrusive thought and draining it of its emotional power, we can discard it and return to the repetition of the Jesus Prayer, cultivating stillness and drawing closer to God.

However, it's important that our desire to grow closer to God should not exceed our capacity to do so. God does not ask us to run faster than our feet will carry us.

Recognizing Our Limitations

As we move from one knot to the next on the komboskini, new thoughts inevitably arise, spinning new narratives. When this happens, we must return to the process of examining them. This practice can be mentally tiring, but like with building physical strength, progress comes with persistence. With consistent daily discipline, we gradually transform ourselves.

It's essential to recognize our limits during each session. The goal is not to feel drained, as if we've subjected our minds to a twelve-round boxing match, but rather to finish with a greater sense of equanimity and peace.

Our purpose is not to achieve a superficial sense of accomplishment by completing multiple cycles of a hundred-knot komboskini. There should be no feeling of pride or accomplishment upon completion of our practice for the day. Using the method I have presented, it might take years to complete even a single cycle of a thirty-three-knot komboskini without being tricked by our minds into spinning a rising thought into an elaborate narrative.

The real task before us is purifying the soul so that we may be conformed to His likeness. Part of this journey involves not only observing our inner thoughts and passions but also realizing that the thoughts and passions of others are not separate from our own. We take them in, and they, too, must be dealt with.

Including All Minds as Our Own

As we address the imperfections in our own glass, we begin to see how our inner state affects our interactions with others. This recognition calls us to include the thoughts and emotions of others in our spiritual practice, recognizing how their struggles and feelings intersect with our own inner experiences.

Addressing only our personal inner thoughts and emotions is not enough to cultivate the equanimity and dispassion I've described; we must also acknowledge how the thoughts, feelings, and actions of others can disturb our peace. By integrating this awareness into our mindfulness and metacognition practices, we train ourselves to respond with calmness and clarity rather than reactive emotion.

Paradoxically, it is through approaching the inner struggles of others with dispassion that we learn to extend true compassion. This dispassion—which is far removed from indifference—becomes the foundation for empathy and love, enabling us to see others not as adversaries but as fellow travelers on the shared journey toward peace. They, too, wrestle with the same inner demons we seek to conquer.

A powerful example of this dynamic is found in Scripture, where our Lord has just told His disciples that He would be rejected by the priests and scribes, delivered unto death, but rise again after three days. Peter, pulling our Lord aside, attempts to rebuke Him, but Christ swiftly and decisively silences him:

Mark 8:32b-33

32b . . . Peter took him [aside] and began to
rebuke him.

33 But Jesus, turning around and seeing his
disciples, rebuked Peter, saying, "Get
behind me, Satan! For you have in mind
not the things of God, but the things of
men."

It is essential to emphasize a point discussed in the chapter "The Serpent": the term "satan" should not be transliterated as the proper name "Satan." Instead, it is more accurately translated as "adversary," and its meaning depends on context. This adversarial role can either serve God's purposes or oppose them.

In this moment, Jesus was not condemning Peter but addressing the nature of his thoughts: "For you have in mind not the things of God." Our Lord treated Peter's expressed thoughts as an extension of His own mind, examining their origin and rendering judgment on them. At the same time, He was guiding Peter in the hesychastic practice of examining his own thoughts to discern their source.

This interaction also reflects how Christ likely approached the thoughts that arose within His own mind. He modeled for us a way to examine not only our personal inner struggles but also the thoughts and actions of others. When others express their thoughts, we must remember that these thoughts are not the eternal essence of the person but transient disturbances—temporary and fleeting—that must be addressed with discernment and compassion.

By following Christ's example, we can approach others' thoughts not as personal attacks but as reflections of their inner struggles. This allows us to respond with clarity and grace, guiding them—and ourselves—toward alignment with God's purposes.

From Awareness to Transformation

True spiritual growth begins with the courage to observe our inner world honestly and with humility. By transitioning from automatic thinking to conscious awareness and metacognition, we take the first steps toward aligning our hearts and minds with God's will.

This journey requires patience and persistence. It is not about achieving perfection in a single moment but about steadily cultivating inner stillness day by day. As we examine our thoughts, naming and disarming those that cling to us, we prepare the soil of our hearts for God's presence. Through this labor, we begin to eat the "daily bread" of His presence, finding life and renewal in Him.

Let us remember that this work is deeply personal, yet never solitary. Each repetition of the Jesus Prayer, each moment of self-awareness, and each effort to cleanse the inner glass brings us closer to becoming a living tabernacle for God. In doing so, we not only transform ourselves but also grow in compassion and love for others, recognizing their struggles as part of our shared human journey.

The path of metacognition, or neptic discernment, is not merely a psychological exercise; it is a spiritual discipline that leads to deeper communion with God. With each thought we confront and release, with every moment of stillness we embrace, we participate in the great work of becoming like Christ, the Dispassionate One.

So let us begin this journey, step by step, thought by thought, with humility and hope, knowing that Christ walks with us and guides us toward the restoration of our inner paradise.

Chapter Twenty-Three

True Holiness

Awareness of Our Motivations

Having explored the practices that cultivate inner purification and illumination, we must also stay watchful for the thorns of false spiritual progress. The pursuit of holiness is often apophatic—shaped as much by what we must avoid as by what we must embrace.

Avoid Outward Displays

Jesus Himself warned against outward displays of piety when He said the following:

> **Matthew 23:5**
>
> 5 Instead, they do all their works to be seen by men. They make their phylacteries broad, they enlarge the fringes of their garments . . .

Each Christian must continuously examine their motives, for even something as seemingly innocent as the choice of a komboskini can become a stumbling block to spiritual growth. Upon reflection, if we find that we are trying to impress others—or even ourselves—we must confront this temptation directly. It's easy to cling to outward acts of piety, especially when we subconsciously seek affirmation through flattery:

Proverbs 29:5

5 A man who flatters his neighbor spreads
a net for his feet.

Flattery, whether from others or ourselves, should always be seen as a snare that leads to our downfall. Awareness of these subtle temptations is essential if we wish to remain focused on our true inner work.

Similarly, even if we don't seek explicit praise from others, we may engage in acts designed to impress others, such as an exaggerated gesture of crossing oneself, bowing much deeper than everyone else, or affecting serene smiles meant to convey inner peace. These behaviors, while often unintentional, can create the illusion of spiritual maturity. When this happens, it can inadvertently slow true growth, as our focus shifts from authentic transformation to maintaining outward displays of holiness. Breaking free from this cycle requires a great deal of awareness, as well as a return to humility.

Our internal adversary is cunning, offering countless false signs of spiritual progress to divert us from the difficult but necessary task of cultivating the inner land. I have mentioned this awareness of our outward displays of piety because this, too, increases our awareness and entrance into metacognition. Indeed, these principles must be applied to every waking thought and action.

These snares don't just include misguided motivations, such as outward displays of piety or reliance on others' praise to affirm spiritual progress. One of the most insidious weeds is the reliance on manufactured feelings as proof of spirituality.

Avoid Manufacturing Feelings of Holiness

It is worth expanding on St. Symeon the New Theologian's insights in this area, which I referenced in the chapter "Obstacles to the Jesus Prayer." Holiness cannot be fabricated through emotions or mental constructs. When we deliberately summon holy images or attempt to impose them upon the soul, we risk engraving external illusions of holiness rather than fostering authentic inner transformation. Such mental imagery can actually disrupt the inner stillness essential for true prayer, acting as an external imposition rather than allowing the Holy Spirit to transform the soul from within.

True holiness—being fully in the Presence of God—can only imprint itself upon the soul when the mind is clear and free from self-generated images and self-constructed feelings. This is not a rejection of icons or holy images in worship; rather, as St. Symeon the New Theologian counsels, in the practice of interior stillness, all external or imagined images must be set aside to allow God to enter the soul without interference. Icons and images help foster a sense of unity and belonging to the same spiritual family along with the saints and Christ. However, for the sake of pure prayer, these symbols must be set aside to nurture inner silence.

Defying Expectations

In *The Ascetical Homilies of St. Isaac the Syrian, Homily 44*, St. Isaac states, "The saints, while still in this world, dwell as if in the tomb, invisible to the world." He emphasizes that true holiness involves deep inner communion with God, which remains largely imperceptible to those around them. Their lives are characterized by obscurity, with their spiritual achievements hidden from public view and detached from worldly recognition.

In other words, a truly spiritual person often defies our expectations of what holiness should look like. Their holiness is not marked by outward displays of piety but by an inward transformation that escapes human notice. Such a person may be the most invisible individual in your parish, living in quiet humility.

Elder Paisios of Mount Athos echoes this emphasis in *Spiritual Counsels, Vol. II: Spiritual Awakening*, teaching, "True spiritual life is hidden. It does not show itself; it does not seek approval." This counsel reinforces the idea that true spiritual growth is an intimate and private journey, one that avoids drawing attention to itself while fostering a deeper relationship with God.

Measuring Holiness by Equanimity and Dispassion

The ultimate measure of progress is what I mentioned earlier: when distracting thoughts and emotions less frequently disrupt our practice of the Jesus Prayer and our everyday thinking. We will know we are making progress when we experience greater calm and equanimity in our daily activities, remaining aware of the thoughts that enter our minds rather than being swept away by elaborating on them. This is a deeply personal transformation—something no one else can observe.

To achieve this level of stillness, the continuous stream of thoughts and images must eventually lose its hold on the mind. The only way to neutralize their grip is to confront them directly. This means not suppressing or avoiding thoughts but fully recognizing and understanding them to strip them of their power. Just as controlled fire can prevent a wildfire, metacognitive thinking—consciously observing and directing one's thoughts—can help subdue the inner noise.

True holiness is not marked by visible signs but by a profound alignment with God's presence, cultivated through humility, stillness, and an unwavering focus on inner transformation. This is why I made the bold assertion earlier that these "advanced" techniques "may be equally, if not more, beneficial for both laypeople and monastics." While continuous repetition of the Jesus Prayer may not be attainable for laypeople preoccupied with work and family life, we all can develop the ability to observe and confront our thoughts with awareness. This transformative practice is open to everyone, regardless of life circumstances.

Steadfastness Builds Holiness

This practice is like cleaning the glass of the soul—rinsing away inner dirt and polishing the surface so thoughts and emotions cling less often. Over time, we increase our ability to perform this exercise without being distracted.

An interesting shift happens during this practice. If we believe the goal is simply repeating the Jesus Prayer and treating distractions as interruptions, we are both right and wrong. The number of knots we reach before a thought arises serves as a measure of progress, but it is not the goal itself.

It's impossible to break the power of these thoughts and passions if we don't understand their origins, emotional pull, or the defects in our souls that attract them. Without these insights, how can we achieve a state of equanimity and dispassion? Reciting the Jesus Prayer without ever engaging in awareness and metacognition keeps us in a state of spiritual blindness. We live and practice without truly seeing or engaging in the inner battlefield that must be conquered for the inner kingdom of heaven to be established.

Repetition is indeed essential, but it's the type of repetition that matters. The cycle of prayer, interrupted by thoughts and images, followed by metacognitive examination and the neutralization of those thoughts, leads to real transformation. This is the true work of spiritual growth, and it is the only repetition that truly matters, for it mirrors the Eastern Orthodox axiom of what our path is all about—it's about falling down and getting up, over and over again.

The more we engage in this transition from automatic thinking to metacognition, the more it will happen throughout our entire day, during every activity. Becoming the observer and abiding in a state of awareness soon becomes more and more frequently our normal state of being.

Restoring Paradise

The ultimate goal of prayer is not just stillness but an ever-deepening communion with God, where the heart becomes pure, free of distractions, and aligned with His will. It is only in this stillness that we truly come to know God. We should recognize that this practice is a lifelong commitment. There is no need to rush or feel anxious about our progress in the spiritual journey; we shouldn't worry about potentially falling short and missing out on future rewards. The reward is right now!

Each day, as our souls become more organized, greater peace reigns, and equanimity gains greater dominion, we are building the kingdom within. All that Christ asks is that we build upon what He has given to each of us, and we do so gradually, step by step, day by day. Being anxious about any of this defeats the purpose of the practice. As soon as you begin, you have won, for Christ will in no wise cast out anyone who is in the process of coming to Him.

This is how we restore ourselves to paradise, to the inner Garden of Eden. It is up to us to till the ground of our inner landscape, preparing the inner kingdom for the coming of our Lord; it is up to us to build up the walls of Jerusalem so that God can come and dwell within as our eternal King of all.

Part Seven

Returning to the Garden

The purpose of this book is to offer a new vision of the Genesis allegories—one seen through the Hebrew language, the Jewish context, and the path of silence. Through these lenses, the reader may approach the Bible with fresh eyes: discovering truths once hidden, raising questions where passages once seemed illogical, and seeing them resolved within a larger framework.

That context is the transformation of man through the gift of the Law and the Presence, leading him from chaos into divine order. Adam and Eve—Man and Life—are allegorical figures pointing to Moses and Israel, and to Christ and the Church. With these truths in mind, all of Scripture comes into focus.

Now we return to the two narratives at the heart of Genesis: *The Creation of Man* and *The Fall of Man*. Their hidden depth emerges when we see them as the story of humanity being shaped into a "man in our image."

First, we will reflect on the moment when God breathed the breath of life into man's nostrils. Then we will consider the mystery of Man and Life hearing the sound—perhaps even the voice—of God walking in the garden in the cool of the day. And woven through both, we will trace a pattern that extends far beyond Eden—a pattern of fall, exile, and restoration that repeated across Israel's history, from Moab to Babylon and beyond, each time the same God approaching the same fallen people with the same breath of life.

Until now, these passages have been set aside, not from lack of importance, but to avoid sacrificing the vision of the forest by dwelling too long among its trees. Here, at last, we pause within the forest's depths to uncover the meaning they conceal.

Chapter Twenty-Four

The Breath of Life

The Instilling of Life

I tend to read the Scriptures with a software engineer's curiosity—always asking why things are the way they are, and how they fit together. This habit naturally leads me to questions like these when I read the following verse:

> **Genesis 2:7**
>
> 7 Then the LORD God formed man of the dust of the ground, and breathed into his nostrils the breath of life; and man became a living soul.

Why does God breathe life into man through the nostrils instead of the mouth? If this were about filling lungs with air, wouldn't the mouth be the more natural path? Or why bother with breath at all? If we follow the literalist's view of this narrative, God spoke the world into existence. Could He not have simply said, "Let man have life!"?

Could the explanation behind this act be directly related to God's desire to make man in His image? If so, in what way?

The Nostrils: More Than a Physical Organ

In Jewish thought, the nostrils were far more than a bodily organ for breathing. They were understood as the seat of passion—specifically, of anger. The Hebrew word used here, *aph* (אַף, ahf), occurs 177 times in the Hebrew Scriptures, and in 104 of those, it refers not to anatomy but to a mental state, usually wrath. We find phrases like *aph Ya'aqov*—literally, "the nose of Jacob," but clearly understood as "the anger of Jacob."[70]

This nuance cannot be ignored when we encounter the term in Genesis 2:7. If the breath of life is infused into the *aph*, the symbolic seat of anger, the verse is doing far more than reporting a biological animation of dust. God breathes into the symbolic hearth of human passion—the threshold of disorder—and claims it as His own.

And when we consider the aim of the Torah—transforming the inner garden of chaos into one ordered by God—the choice to breathe into the nostrils becomes deeply significant. It is not incidental. God breathes His life into the center of wrath, reclaiming that space as His own. Into the very place where ungoverned emotion would otherwise reside, God breathes His own breath—what we have already seen throughout Scripture to symbolize both His Law and Presence.

The Symbolism of Divine Patience

Even the idiom for God's mercy affirms this symbolism. In Psalm 103:8, we read: *erekh apayim*—"slow to anger," literally "long of nostrils." The image is striking: short nostrils suggest hot breath and quick temper, while long nostrils cool the heat and delay reaction.

The metaphor reflects lived experience. Anger quickens our breathing, flares our nostrils, and sends heat across the face. To describe God as "long of nostrils" is to say: His breath is not rash, His passion not uncontrolled, His presence measured and patient.

---

[70] Genesis 30:2

And what God breathes into man is not the quick flare of wrath but the steadying power of His Law and Presence.

A Declaration of Inner Peace

This symbolism finds its most poignant expression in the words of Job:

Job 27:3

3 All the while my breath is in me, and
the spirit of God is in my nostrils.

Job does not mean merely that he still breathes. He means that even in the collapse of his life—his children, wealth, health, and even God's favor—something remains unshaken.

The divine breath is still in him. His nostrils—the seat of wrath—still carry the Spirit of God. Though his world is in ruins, the sanctuary within is unbroken. His lips do not curse, his silence is not overcome by chaos.

This is a hesychastic victory: the very place of wrath remains a temple of presence. It is Job's testimony, his defiance of despair: even here, even now, God's Spirit remains in my breath.

Law and Presence: A Sacred Infusion

The two gifts—Law and Presence—are the foundation of the journey into hesychia, the silence in which humanity is transformed and comes to know God. And where does this journey begin? In the very place once ruled by wrath.

The breath of God is not simply the spark of animation; it is a sanctifying act, reclaiming the seat of passion itself. The nostrils, once flaring with chaos, are made channels of divine stillness.

From here the path unfolds: the fire of wrath is cooled, silence descends, and the garden within—once overrun by the thorns and thistles of disorder—is restored to God.

Layers of Meaning

Did the author of Genesis consciously intend every layer of this symbolism? Perhaps not. But I believe the Author behind the author(s) did. Any God-inspired work is filled with layer upon layer, meaning upon meaning, beyond even what its human writer can see. Even he, returning to his own work, may find himself astonished at depths he had not known were there.

The Scriptures speak with both literal and symbolic voices, and to ignore the symbolic is to miss their fullness. These narratives are not only history but allegory—stories of transformation. God breathes into dust and makes it His own. He breathes into Jacob, leads him to Sinai, and gives him both Law and Presence.

And when Jacob squandered that breath—when the Temple fell and the Torah was lost and the people were carried to Babylon—God breathed it back. He restored the Torah through Ezra's public reading. He restored the Presence through the rebuilding of the Temple. The pattern did not end at Sinai or Moab; it continued through exile and return, each iteration confirming that the breath of life is not a singular event but God's recurring act of mercy toward a people who keep forgetting how to breathe.

In Christ, the pattern is recapitulated: just as Moses received the Law and the Presence on the mountain, so Christ embodies and bestows them in fullness. As John records:

John 20:22

22 And when he had said this, he breathed on them and told them, "Receive the Holy Spirit."

Here Christ accomplishes what Moses only foreshadowed—He transmits Law and Presence in a way that truly transforms His disciples, not merely instructs them. In this single allegory, two stories converge: the life of Israel under Moses and the twelve tribes, and the life of the Church under Christ and the twelve apostles.

The pattern remains constant: the breath of life is Law and Presence. The breathing of these two into Jacob's seat of passion and anger was God's act of shaping a man in His image.

Chapter Twenty-Five

Restoring the Breath

Israel's Estrangement

After God breathed life into Man, rebellion soon followed, and he ceased to be a man in His image. His brief inhalation of divine likeness was followed by a long exhalation of estrangement, leaving him empty.

Allegory, by its nature, layers history upon history. A single episode in Israel's life may inspire the narrative, yet the same motifs echo across generations, reappearing whenever God's people fall and are cast from His presence. So it is with the story of Eden.

I have argued that *The Fall of Man* reflects Israel's sojourn in the plains of Moab, when they bowed to the daughters of Moab and fell into idolatry. The setting of that fall was described by Balaam in Edenic imagery: "As valleys stretched out, as gardens by the river-side; as aloes planted of the LORD, as cedars beside the waters;".[71]

Yet that was not the only fall. Israel would be cast out again and again—into Assyrian exile, Babylonian captivity, and finally at the destruction of the Second Temple. The allegory applies in every case: estrangement from God always leads to expulsion from the garden. And for us as well: when we bow to idols, we step outside His Presence.

---

[71] Numbers 24:6

Breathing Life into the Ruins

Of all these exiles, the Babylonian captivity stands as the most devastating and the most instructive. For a generation, the children of Israel lived without the Temple, without organized public worship, and in many cases without access to the Torah itself. The institutions that had defined them as God's people—the priesthood, the sacrificial system, the liturgical calendar, the very land promised to Abraham—had been stripped away. They were, in the fullest sense, east of Eden, expelled from the place of God's presence, just as both Adam[72] and Cain[73] were driven eastward after their falls.

After slaying his brother, Cain was exiled from God's presence and received a mark to preserve his life — a sign of mercy extended even to the fallen. Centuries later, Ezekiel, himself living in exilic Babylon, saw a vision of a man clothed in linen marking the foreheads of the contrite with a *tav* — in the ancient script, an X — to spare them during the destruction of Jerusalem,[74] in essence, marking contrition as the single virtue that opens the door through which grace enters and restoration begins.

Yet even in that desolation, God had not abandoned them. The pattern we have traced throughout this book—fall, exile, contrition, restoration—was about to repeat itself once more.

When the remnant returned to Jerusalem, they found the Temple in ruins and the rhythm of worship silenced. But what

---

[72] Genesis 3:24

[73] Genesis 4:16

[74] Ezekiel 9:4. - *Once again, God distinguished those who grieved over the nation's sins and placed His protective mark upon them. We must ask: Did Ezekiel's vision, born from the lived experience of exile, feed back into the Genesis narratives that were taking shape in that same period? It is also worth noting that the mark of the beast in Revelation (13:16–17; 14:9) may be understood as the deliberate inversion of this mark — placed on the same location, the forehead, but sealing allegiance to a counterfeit authority rather than contrition before God. Where the tav, symbolic of contrition, opens the door to grace, the beast's mark of open rebellion closes it.*

followed was nothing less than a national resurrection. The Temple was rebuilt, and when its foundation was laid, the people wept and shouted simultaneously—the old who remembered the former glory mourning what had been lost, the young rejoicing at what was being restored.

The restoration deepened when Ezra the scribe stood before the assembled people and read the Torah publicly—perhaps for the first time in a generation. The book of the Law, which had earlier been discovered by the priest Hilkiah during Josiah's reign was now restored to the center of Israel's life. And when the people heard the words of the Law, they wept:

Nehemiah 8:9

9 And Nehemiah, who was the Tirshatha, and Ezra the priest the scribe, and the Levites that taught the people, said unto all the people: 'This day is holy unto the Lord your God; mourn not, nor weep.' For all the people wept, when they heard the words of the Law.

Consider what occurred in that moment through the lens this book has developed. The two components of the breath of life—the Torah and the Presence—were precisely what had been lost in the exile and precisely what was now being restored. The Torah, forgotten or inaccessible for decades, was read aloud and received with contrition. The Temple, destroyed by Nebuchadnezzar, was rebuilt and its worship reconstituted. Together, these constituted God's breath entering the nostrils of His people once again—into the very seat of the passions that had led them into idolatry—restoring them as a man made in His image.

The people's weeping at the reading of the Law mirrors the experience of Man and Life after their eyes were opened. They recognized their nakedness—their spiritual condition—and mourned. Their contrition was real, even if imperfect, even if mingled with the relief of survival and the anxiety of rebuilding.

And God, in His mercy, did not wait until the garden within was fully restored. He came while it was still in ruins, while the walls of Jerusalem were still broken, while the people still bore the marks of their years among foreign gods. He received them as they were and began again the work of transformation.

This is the same pattern we see enacted earlier, in the plains of Moab, where the restoration was no less dramatic and no less instructive.

In Moab, the rebellion was stark. Israel had just suffered plague for their idolatry when Zimri publicly defied God by bringing a Midianite woman into his tent. Phinehas struck them down, and the plague ceased. What followed was restoration: a new census to confirm the death of the old generation, inheritance laws to prepare for the land, and a recitation of the calendar of offerings to reestablish the rhythm of worship. These were not random commands. They were God's way of breathing life back into His people, resuscitating Israel as a man in His image.

We have now seen the same pattern enacted twice in Israel's history — once after the exile, once in Moab. What the Genesis narrative does is distill this recurring rhythm into a single story, compressing centuries of fall and restoration into the encounter between God and two figures in a garden. What follows in the text is not one event but every event of its kind, rendered in the language of allegory.

This is the setting leading up to Genesis 3:8, where God's voice is heard in the garden, seeking to restore communion once again.

The Voice of God in the Garden

Sensing the loss of inward fruit, they sought to imitate it outwardly—clothing themselves with leaves as though appearance could replace substance. It was in this state that God found them, as the text next records:

Genesis 3:8

8 And they heard the voice of the LORD God walking in the garden toward the cool of the day . . .

At first glance, the wording feels strange. Can a voice really walk? Some translators smooth this by rendering it, "the sound of the Lord God walking." The Hebrew word *qol* (קוֹל, KOHL) can indeed mean either "voice" or "sound." But even then, how could footsteps be heard in a garden? Eden had no stone floors where echoes might ring out. The problem is heightened when many translations speak of the "breezy time of the day" rather than the "cool of the day." In such a setting, the rustling leaves would have made footsteps nearly impossible to hear.

The Hebrew points us toward something deeper. The word translated "walking" is *mithallekh* (מתהלך, meet-ha-LEKH), which means moving about, walking back and forth. Yet this root (*halakh*) conveys more than just motion. It later led to the word *halakhah*—"the way of walking"—which came to describe living according to God's instruction. And as we saw in Chapter Seven, the word Torah itself comes from another root (*yarah*), which means *to point out the way*.

Taken together, these words give the verse a richer meaning. What Man and Life heard was not merely the sound of footsteps among the rustling leaves. They sensed the presence of God, which pointed them back to the path they had abandoned. He was seeking once again to breathe His stillness, His Law, and His Presence into the very seat of their passions, their rebellion.

Here is the echo of Genesis 2:7: the breath of life granted to Israel at Mount Sinai, seeking to create a man in His image, returns to once again breathe life into a new generation of the children of Israel. They were being made ready; they had observed a time of national mourning at the Tent of Meeting, a contrition—however mixed—that alone could invite back the Presence of God. Their eyes were open; they were ready to both see and hear.

We do not know how pure their contrition truly was. Did they mourn because they had offended God, or because their loved ones lay dead? Was it sorrow for sin, or fear lest they too be condemned? Perhaps it was both. Yet even such imperfect grief was enough for God. For contrition need not be flawless; it need only soften the soil of the heart so that the rain of His Presence may seep into the ground. God does not wait until the garden within is perfectly restored, until the inner kingdom stands complete and unshaken. He comes while it is still in ruins, if only He finds us willing. There, amid the rubble, He begins the work of rebuilding, until what was desolate becomes again a dwelling fit for His Presence.

The Disguise of Leaves

After their eyes were opened, Man and Life sewed fig leaves together to cover themselves. This detail, often regarded as incidental or a symbol of shame, deserves closer examination. Fig leaves are broad and large, forming a sort of canopy. By sewing them together, Man and Life did more than just cover their bodies. Whether consciously or not, they were creating a new image of themselves, one that would blend back into the garden.

The leaves signified more than concealment; they expressed the paradox of the human heart. On the one hand, there was contrition — an awareness of their nakedness and the loss of innocence. On the other hand, there was the impulse to preserve appearance, to be seen as pious, to clothe failure in signs of reverence. The leaves became the first attempt at religion: outward observance reaching toward God, yet mingled with the instinct to hide.

So too with Israel. At the Tent of Meeting, their mourning was real. Yet their sorrow was expressed through outward observances — gathering, weeping, offerings — that also carried the human desire to appear righteous before others. Outward appearance and inward contrition lived side by side, as they still do in every age. We know we are inwardly naked, but we don't want others to see that nakedness, and so we clothe ourselves in the appearance of fruitfulness. This is a well-known phenomenon in psychology called *symbolic self-completion*, where people adopt outward symbols to represent a desired identity when they haven't achieved it genuinely.

This paradox is why the fig tree becomes such a fitting symbol. Jesus approached it expecting fruit, but found only leaves. It was clothed in outward signs of life, but inwardly barren. So it was with Man and Life: their leaves were both the sign of their turning and the sign of their disguise. The danger is not in outward observance itself — which can rightly express repentance — but in relying on leaves without fruit, appearance without substance.

Hiding Among the Fruitful

The text next says they hid themselves "amongst the ***trees*** of the garden" (JPS 1917), *bethokh ets haggan* (בתוך עץ הגן, beh-TOHCH EYTS hah-GAHN). Yet this is a "corrected" translation, since the Hebrew does not say "trees" (*ʿēṣîm*) but "tree" (*ʿēṣ*). Most translators smooth the text as though it must describe a physical hiding place. But if we leave the Hebrew as it stands—"amongst the ***tree*** of the garden"—it opens a different picture altogether.

Which tree could this be? Earlier in Genesis, two trees stood in the midst of the garden: the Tree of Life and the Tree of the

Knowledge of Good and Evil. Since Man and Life had just eaten from the latter, their hiding may be read as taking refuge in the very principle they had just embraced: self-guided wisdom in place of communion with God. In this sense, "the tree" is not a literal covering but the idolatry of choosing for themselves which voice to follow.

If so, their hiding takes on a deeper meaning. Having lost the fruits of virtue, they turned to appearances — outward tokens that resembled life while concealing their true nature. Their attempt to hide was not only excuse-making, but also the instinct to present themselves as still belonging in the garden, while leaning on the false security of their own judgment.

What happens in Eden is not an isolated act of hiding, but a pattern that later reappears in Israel's own story. In the plains of Moab, after the plague, they gathered at the Tent of Meeting. Their mourning was genuine, yet it was also expressed through external acts of piety. Now, there was another strong motivation for this outward display: they had just seen an unknown number of their fellow citizens executed by the judges for committing a serious sin. Perhaps, they wanted to show they were remorseful and not in agreement with those who were condemned.

Here too, contrition and appearance lived side by side, as they do here in Eden. To hide "among the tree" is to take refuge in a form of life — observance, ritual, pretense — or in the idol of one's own self-chosen wisdom, while the substance of communion has been lost, but being earnestly sought.

The Breath of the Day

And so, into this hiding place—into the shadow of excuses, self-justification, and idolatry—comes the voice of God. The text continues by telling us they heard the voice of God walking in the garden "toward the cool of the day," *leruach hayyom* (לרוח היום, leh-ROO-ahch hah-YOHM).

Most modern translations render this as "in the cool of the day," but the Hebrew uses the preposition *le*, meaning "toward." Scholars note that this time of day likely refers to the evening breeze. Yet in Hebrew thought, *'erev*—evening—means more than a time of day. It signifies mixture, confusion, the creeping in of chaos.[75] One might ask, How is the evening breeze the harbinger of the approaching chaos? The text is not painting a scene of weather alone; it is signaling a turning point in creation, a shift from stillness toward disorder.

The evening breeze stirred the leaves, breaking the stillness with its gentle rustling. This rising murmur, a precursor to nightfall, symbolizes the shift from silence into noise, from order into the first traces of chaos. It was in this moment—before darkness fully descended—that God approached Man and Life, calling them back to repentance. The narrative is subtle here: just as the world teeters toward confusion, God steps in, moving toward His creatures with calm intention.

His voice moves "toward the cool of the day"—toward the breeze that signals night's arrival—not to be drowned in its noise, but to bring stillness in its midst. He enters the moment when disorder is about to swallow creation, and He does so as peace, inviting Man and Life to return before the darkness closes in.

This draws us back to *The Creation of Man*, where God breathed into Man's nostrils, the seat of passion and anger, the breath of life, thereby transforming him into His image. That same breath, once rejected, now comes again. What was first given for communion is now heard as an invitation, calling them back to the life they had abandoned. In both instances, Genesis 2:7 and 3:8, God is introducing His stillness into the heart of the chaotic breezes of self-guidance that disturb man's soul.

---

[75] See Chapter Six, Before the Light

Even here, there is mercy. The voice does not pursue in wrath. It walks. It draws near. It gives them space to confess—to show the sacrifice God desires most: contrition.

Clothed in What They Had Become

The Scriptures say that God "clothed them in garments of skin" *vayyalbishem* (וילבשם, vah-yahl-bee-SHEYM). The Hebrew Hiphil form is usually causative, but it can also carry a permissive sense. To take it strictly as causative would suggest that God Himself wrapped Man and Life in corruption, making Him the author of sin. Yet the permissive nuance allows another reading: He permitted them to be clothed in what they had already embraced inwardly, once His glory was withdrawn.

Perhaps there were literal garments of skin, but the narrative presses us to see them chiefly as signs. The skins became outward tokens of the passions in which they had clothed themselves. Innocence once robed them; now appetite and disorder did. In this way, the garments are not instruments of sin imposed by God, but symbols of what humanity had already chosen.

The narrative here gives us the first glimpse of a recurring biblical principle: God does not impose corruption, but permits men to remain in what they have chosen. —a pattern that recurs throughout Israel's story: God "hardened Pharaoh's heart,"[76] not by creating evil within him, but by permitting him to persist in his stubbornness. God allowed "a lying spirit"[77] to deceive Ahab's prophets, not by authoring deceit, but by giving Ahab over to the falsehood he loved.

These later echoes show that the principle established in Eden continued to shape Israel's history. So too here: the skins are

---

[76] Exodus 4:21; 7:3; 9:12

[77] 1 Kings 22:23

permitted as outward signs of what Man and Life had become, not as corruption forced upon them by God. Thus, the garments serve both as narrative detail and allegory: a literal covering, yet also a spiritual symbol. They mark the turn from innocence to passion, from transparency to concealment. And they prepare the long path of return, where skins must at last be laid aside before one may tread on holy ground again.

But the garments can also be seen as an act of compassion. Man and Life no longer stood unashamedly naked before Him, having nothing to hide. Their fig leaves of excuse had been stripped away, yet God did not leave them exposed in shame. Instead, He received them as they were—clothed in the tokens of their fallen passions—and began again with them. It was a beginning marked not by innocence but by mercy, just as He found Jacob in the wilderness, as *The Song of Moses* recalls: "He found him in a desert land . . . He compassed him about, He cared for him, He kept him as the apple of His eye."[78]

To begin again, Man had to stand before God acknowledging his condition: no longer innocent, but carnal; no longer in the rhythm of worship, but clothed in beastly passions. In that sense, the garments of skin were a new form of nakedness—an admission: "I acknowledge before You my true nature, without pretense or further excuse." God transforms no one who will not first confess the depth of their fall.

The same truth echoes at Pentecost:

Acts 2:37

37 Now when the people heard this, they were cut to the heart and asked Peter

[78] Deuteronomy 32:10

> and the rest of the apostles, "Brethren,
> what shall we do?"

No man can re-enter God's presence until he is cut to the heart in the same way, stripped of excuse and standing bare before Him. So too with Israel: their day of national mourning at the Tent of Meeting proved they were ready. Contrition prepared the soil, and God, seeing their repentance, breathed His order back into them.

From Skins to Sandals

The thread runs further through Scripture. Israel, like Man and Life, later clothed itself again in the passions of Egypt after tasting God's presence. And when Moses approached the burning bush, God commanded him: "put off thy shoes from off thy feet, for the place whereon thou standest is holy ground."[79] The sandals were literal coverings, but they were also signs. Made of animal skins, they symbolized the lower nature, the passions bound to mortality. To step upon holy ground, Moses had to cast them off. What had served as practical protection now stood as a barrier between the man and God's presence.

Here, the pattern becomes clear. In Eden, humanity was permitted to be clothed in skins, outward tokens of an inward fall. In Midian, Moses was commanded to remove skins from his feet, outward tokens of a necessary purification. The journey from fig leaves to animal skins to bare feet is both literal and allegorical: from pretense, to passion, to purification—from rebellion, to repentance, to return.

This movement—begun in Eden, carried forward in Moses, and repeated across Israel's history—prepares the way for the greater return in Christ.

---

[79] Exodus 3:5

Guarded From the Tree of Life

The narrative does not end with the garments of skin. Another detail presses the point further:

Genesis 3:22-23

22 And the LORD God said: "Behold, the man is become as one of us, to know good and evil; and now, lest he put forth his hand, and take also of the tree of life, and eat, and live for ever."

23 Therefore the LORD God sent him forth from the garden of Eden, to till the ground from whence he was taken.

Here, the structure of the text matters. Verse 22 is not a finished sentence in itself. It is all protasis—" lest he put forth his hand . . ."—with no expressed conclusion. The apodosis comes in the very next verse: "Therefore the LORD God sent him forth . . ." The expulsion is the answer to the concern.

But what exactly was the concern? The usual reading assumes that Man was in possession of immortality, and that God feared he might seize it permanently. Yet the Hebrew word *le'olam* (לעלם, leh-oh-LAHM) does not mean "forever" in the Greek metaphysical sense of eternity. It means "for an age," an indefinite but lengthy span of time. What God was preventing was not man's possession of divine immortality, but his prolonging of existence in a distorted condition. In other words, the barrier is not to eternal life itself, but to the endless extension of a corrupted one.

The Tree of Life, as the rest of Scripture shows, is a type of the Torah itself.[80] To stretch out the hand to that tree while still clinging to the Tree of Knowledge was to try to continue in a false

---

[80] Proverbs 3:18; 11:30; 13:12; 15:4

union: enjoying the fruit of Torah outwardly while inwardly bound to idolatry and self-justification. To "eat and live forever," in the original Hebrew, conveys the idea of living indefinitely in that hypocrisy.

This, God would not permit. To be sustained by His Torah while despising His Presence would make rebellion appear as righteousness, idolatry appear as fruitfulness. Thus, He casts Man and Life out of the garden. Exile itself becomes the remedy: the false union is cut short, and man is made to till the ground until repentance prepares the soil of the soul once again. Exile, then, is not punishment for its own sake but medicine—a painful cure meant to restore the possibility of true communion.

The very concern expressed in Eden—that man might cling to life outwardly while estranged inwardly—reappears in Israel's wilderness test. At Peor, they sought to stretch out both hands—to the gods of Moab on the one side, and to the offerings of YHWH on the other. But God's answer was the same as in Eden: "They cannot live in My Presence and simultaneously in willful rebellion." His people cannot eat from the Tree of Life while bowing before the tree of their own choosing.

To be barred from the Tree of Life, then, is not to lose metaphysical eternity, but to lose the pretense of life with God without obedience to God. True eternal life is not endless duration but communion with Him who alone is immortal.[81] That communion cannot be entered while the soul stretches one hand to the Torah and the other to idols.

Yet even as the way was closed to hypocrisy, the way of return was not destroyed. What was denied to rebellion was preserved for repentance. And it is here that the story turns—from exile and barring, to breath and invitation, which is what was truly

---

[81] 1 Timothy 6:16

happening when God walked toward them in the breezy, noisy time of the day that precedes the darkness of chaos.

The Path Back

Thus, the breath of God—once resisted—remains the very means of our return, the same breath that first formed a man in His image. For the Spirit still walks in the garden, calling not only to Man and Life, but to each of us who hide among the trees.

The pattern has never changed. At Sinai, God breathed the Law and His Presence into Jacob, and a people were formed in His image. In Moab, after they fell into idolatry, He restored the rhythm of worship and prepared them to cross into the Promised Land. After the Babylonian exile, when the Torah had been lost and the Temple lay in ruins, He breathed life back through Ezra's reading and the rebuilding of His dwelling place. And at Pentecost, Christ breathed on His disciples and said, "Receive the Holy Spirit"—transmitting the same Law and Presence in their fullness, not merely as instruction but as transformation.

Four times the breath entered. Four times the nostrils—the seat of human wrath and passion—were reclaimed as channels of divine stillness. Four rivers flowing from one garden, carrying the seed of God's word to all the earth.

The journey begins with breath. The nostrils once flared in wrath must become still again. In prayer, the breath is given back to its source. There, in the garden of the soul, silence descends and fruit is restored.

And even now, in the cool of the day, the voice of God still walks—softly, yet insistently—asking the question that has never ceased to echo: "Where are you?"

Endnotes

Scripture Translation Choices:

Unless otherwise noted, Old Testament verses are from the Jewish Publication Society (JPS) 1917 Tanakh, which balances linguistic accuracy and readability while remaining faithful to the Masoretic Text. The JPS 1917 often preserves the cultural and geographical nuances of Hebrew better than many modern translations. All New Testament verses are from the Eastern Orthodox Bible (EOB) 2011, reflecting Eastern Orthodoxy's textual and theological traditions.

Epigenetic Transmission of Stress and Trauma Across Generations

Yehuda, Rachel, Nikolaos P. Daskalakis, Linda M. Bierer, Heather N. Bader, Torsten Klengel, Florian Holsboer, and Elisabeth B. Binder. "Holocaust Exposure Induced Intergenerational Effects on FKBP5 Methylation." Biological Psychiatry 80, no. 5 (September 1, 2016): 372-380.

Costa, Dora L., Noelle Yetter, and Heather DeSomer. "Intergenerational transmission of paternal trauma among US Civil War ex-POWs." Proceedings of the National Academy of Sciences 115, no. 44 (2018): 11215-11220.

Glossary

This glossary includes only foreign terms utilized in multiple sections, making it potentially difficult to find their original in-line definitions.

Term Usage

Foreign words, which are predominantly Hebrew and Greek, are typically presented in the format:

transliteration	(foreign word,	pronunciation guide)
badal	(בדל,	bah-DAHL)

This format is used only for the first mention of each term, where its meaning and pronunciation are explained. Afterward, the transliterated form is used alone, with the expectation that readers will remember the pronunciation if they find it significant. To aid in a proper reading of the pronunciation guide, the "KH" sound resembles the gentle, guttural sound in the German words "ich" or "machen," while the "CH" sound is deeper and more pronounced, like the guttural sound in "Bach" or "loch."

For Greek terms, the pronunciation guide approximates modern Greek pronunciation, which is used in Eastern Orthodoxy when reading ancient Greek texts. Foreign terms that recur throughout the book are italicized and included in the Glossary for convenient reference.

Terms

'eden (עדן, EY-dehn)

This Hebrew word is etymologically derived from the Sumerian word eden, meaning "plain" or "steppe," but is transliterated in the Scriptures as "Eden."

Adam (אדם, ah-DAHM)

A Hebrew word often transliterated as "Adam" but more accurately translated as "Man" or "mankind."

Adam (Ἀδάμ, ah-THAM)

A Greek name transliterated from the Hebrew Adam (אדם, ah-DAHM), as shown above.

Adialeiptos (ἀδιαλείπτως, ah-thee-ah-LEEP-tos)

A Greek word used in Paul's writings, it is translated as "without ceasing" in 1 Thessalonians 5:17. However, Romans 1:9 clarifies its meaning to mean "continual" rather than "continuous" (nonstop).

Akantha (ἄκανθα, AH-kahn-thah)

A Greek term meaning "thorn," equivalent to the Hebrew Qotz.

Avad (עבד, ah-VAHD)

A Hebrew verb meaning "to till," carrying the deeper meaning of "service" and "worship."

Badal (בדל, bah-DAHL)

A Hebrew word meaning "to divide" or "to separate." It is specifically used to describe the separation of the holy from the profane.

Dardar (דרדר, dahr-DAHR)

A Hebrew term meaning "thistle."

Davaq (דבק, dah-VAHK)

A Hebrew word meaning "to cleave," used in Genesis when God commands Adam to cleave to Eve and when the children of Israel are encouraged to cleave to obedience in order to have life.

Dis legomenon (δίς λεγόμενον, DEES leg-OM-enon)

A Greek term referring to a word that appears only twice in a text or corpus.

Esev (עשב, EY-sehv)

A Hebrew word meaning "herbs."

Gezerah shavah (גזירה שוה, geh-zee-RAH shah-VAH)

A Hebrew word that refers to a Talmudic method of Scripture interpretation, which connects separate passages based on shared words or phrases.

Halakhah (הלכה, hah-lah-KHAH)

A Hebrew word meaning "the walk" or "the way," it refers to the oral and written teachings, including Torah and rabbinic interpretations, that guide Jewish law and daily life. It serves as the framework for ethical and religious practice in Judaism.

Hesychia (ἡσυχία, EE-see-CHEE-ah)

A Greek term meaning "stillness" or "quiet." In Eastern Orthodox spirituality, it denotes the path to inner stillness, encompassing purification, illumination, and ultimately union with God (theosis).

Khava (חוה, khah-VAH)

A Hebrew name meaning "Life" that is derived from the root chayah (חיה, khah-YAH), which means "to live." The name signifies Eve's role as the "mother of all living" (Genesis 3:20). In the Septuagint, the name was transliterated into Greek as Εὕα (Euá, ev-AH), which later became "Eve" in English.

Iesous (Ἰησοῦς, ee-SOOS)

The Greek name Iesous is transliterated into English as both "Jesus" and "Joshua." These names are derived from the Aramaic Yeshua (ישוע, yeh-shoo-AH) and the Hebrew Yehoshua (יהושע, yeh-hoh-shoo-AH), respectively. Both forms trace back to the Hebrew root yasha (ישע, yash-AH), meaning "to save" or "to deliver." This name carries the meaning "Yahweh saves" or "salvation of the Lord."

Leitourgia (λειτουργία, lee-toor-GEE-ah)

A Greek word meaning "public service," transliterated into "Liturgy," a worship service within the Orthodox tradition.

Leminah (למינה, leh-mee-NAH)

A Hebrew phrase meaning "after its/their kind," primarily used to categorize living creatures. However, its frequent occurrences in Leviticus and Deuteronomy strongly associate it with the distinction between clean and unclean animals.

Monē (μονή, moh-NEE)

A Greek term meaning "abode" or "dwelling place." It appears only twice in the New Testament, both in John 14.

Nakhash (נחש, nah-KHAHSH)

A Hebrew word meaning "serpent," first used in the narrative of The Fall of Mankind to describe the creature that tempts Eve. Additionally, Nakhash is used as the name of an Ammonite king who opposed Israel.

Qavah (קוה, kah-VAH)

A Hebrew passive verb meaning "to be gathered" that emphasizes an orderly separation, contrasting with the initial chaos of creation.

Qotz (קוץ, KOHTS)

A Hebrew term meaning "thorn."

Rakhaf (רחף, rah-KHAHF)

A Hebrew verb meaning "to hover over," used as one of the inclusios to tie the Song of Solomon to The Creation of Sky and Land allegory.

Satan (שטן, sah-TAHN)

Satan is a Hebrew word meaning "adversary." In the Hebrew Bible, it refers to a role rather than a specific entity and is context-dependent. The term itself is neutral, with its moral connotation—good or evil—determined by the adversary's role in the narrative. Over time, Satan has been transliterated as "Satan," leading to the later theological understanding of a single, malevolent entity, which differs from its original usage.

Sheretz (שרץ, SHEH-rehts)

A Hebrew term meaning "swarm," sometimes used in the same context as Leminah, "after its/their kind"—both used in the context of identifying "clean" and "unclean" creatures.

Siakh (שיח, SEE-ahkh)

A Hebrew word meaning "shrub."

Sola Scriptura

A Latin phrase meaning "Scripture alone," referring to the Protestant belief that the Bible is the sole and ultimate authority in all matters of Christian faith and practice, surpassing church tradition and extra-biblical teachings.

Theosis (θέωσις, THEH-oh-sees)

A Greek term referring to the process of becoming like God through participation in His divine nature. Central to Eastern Orthodox theology, it is the ultimate goal of Christian life, achieved through purification, illumination, and union with God.

Tohu (תהו, TOH-hoo)

A Hebrew word with a range of meanings, including "emptiness," "waste," "desert," "chaos," and "confusion."

Tribolos (τρίβολος, TREE-voh-lohs)

A Greek word meaning "thistle," equivalent to the Hebrew Dardar.

Tsela (צלע, tsey-LAH)

A Hebrew word, translated in the creation narrative as "rib," but significantly translated as "side" when used to describe the Tabernacle and Solomon's Temple.

Yabashah (יבשה, yah-bah-SHAH)

The Hebrew word for "dry land," it symbolizes a place of safety and stability, in contrast to chaotic waters.

Author
Ron Grimes

I encountered Eastern Orthodox Christianity at the age of sixty, after a long and intricate spiritual journey. Raised in the Baptist tradition, I explored various Protestant denominations, delved into Zen Buddhism, and spent a period in atheism before returning to Christianity. Confronted by the diversity of Christian interpretations, I undertook an in-depth study of biblical languages and the Jewish context of Scripture in search of clarity and renewed understanding.

Over the years, I immersed myself in biblical studies, completing five years in Hebrew, one year in Aramaic, and three years in Greek, along with courses on the Jewish context, the geography of Israel, and advanced modern Hebrew. This educational path ultimately led me to the Eastern Orthodox Church, where I discovered the ancient tradition I had been seeking—faith rooted in an unbroken lineage of bishops tracing back to the apostles.

While I have studied extensively at the Israel Institute of Biblical Studies, I hold no formal theological degrees and am not affiliated with the clergy. As a simple parishioner, I am as surprised as anyone by the insights I share in this book. Whether these ideas are the fruits of study or a gift of grace, I leave it for the reader to decide.

For over forty years, I have worked as a software engineer, valuing ideas and innovation over titles or credentials. In this spirit, I hope this book stands on its own merits, inviting readers to view the allegories of creation, the Fall, and perhaps the entire Bible through a new and enlightening lens.

www.ingramcontent.com/pod-product-compliance
Lightning Source LLC
LaVergne TN
LVHW090555110826
845146LV00001B/134

* 9 7 9 8 9 9 2 2 8 2 3 8 2 *